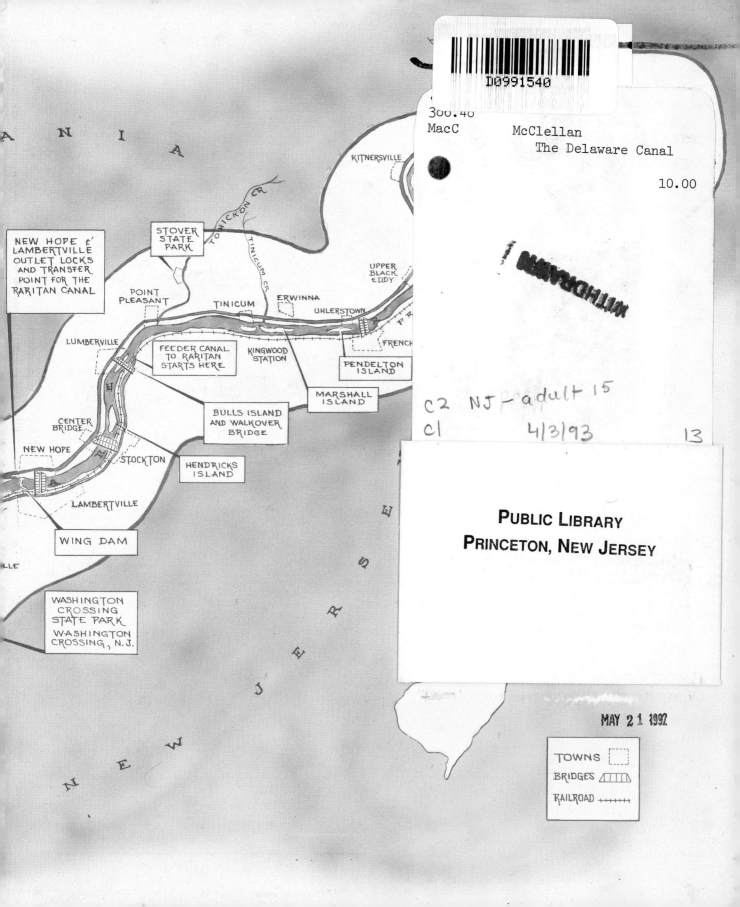

P E N N S Y L V A N I A

N E W   J E R S E Y

KITNERSVILLE

TOHICKON CR.

TINICUM CR.

NEW HOPE & LAMBERTVILLE OUTLET LOCKS AND TRANSFER POINT FOR THE RARITAN CANAL

STOVER STATE PARK

POINT PLEASANT

TINICUM

ERWINNA

UPPER BLACK EDDY

UHLERSTOWN

FRENCH

LUMBERVILLE

FEEDER CANAL TO RARITAN STARTS HERE

KINGWOOD STATION

PENDELTON ISLAND

CENTER BRIDGE

BULLS ISLAND AND WALKOVER BRIDGE

MARSHALL ISLAND

NEW HOPE

STOCKTON

HENDRICKS ISLAND

LAMBERTVILLE

WING DAM

WASHINGTON CROSSING STATE PARK
WASHINGTON CROSSING, N.J.

TOWNS ☐
BRIDGES ⊞
RAILROAD +++++

The Delaware Canal

A Picture Story

THE DELAWARE CANAL

A Picture Story

by

ROBERT J. McCLELLAN

RUTGERS UNIVERSITY PRESS

New Brunswick   *New Jersey*

Foreword

The history of Pennsylvania's once extensive canal system began almost with the settlement of the Colony. As early as 1690, William Penn conceived a plan to construct a series of canals radiating from Philadelphia as a means of transportation and communication by which the western and northern frontiers of the new Colony could be developed. George Washington, in his early exploratory trips into the country which now forms the southwestern part of Pennsylvania, also recognized the need for good transportation routes into this then vast wilderness area.

With the discovery of coal about 1770, in what was to become known as the "Anthracite Region" of Pennsylvania, and its rapid acceptance for use as a prime fuel, tremendous impetus was given to the development of an adequate transportation system by which this important new commodity could be distributed throughout the expanding and developing young nation and, in fact, to foreign markets as well. Pennsylvania, along with other States in the area, began a massive canal construction program, and appointed a Board of Canal Commissioners to develop this transportation system. A network of canals, eventually extending for almost one thousand miles into all sections of the Commonwealth, was constructed and placed in operation.

The Delaware Division Canal, commonly known as the "Delaware Canal," was an important link in this canal system and for more than one hundred years was a vital transportation artery in the Delaware Valley. The men who built it and the boatmen, lock tenders, and other canalers who used, operated and maintained it were a hardy, robust lot who made an indelible impression on the entire region, and left us with a rich heritage of tradition and folklore. But, with the expansion of railroad and highway systems, canal transportation soon became obsolete and by 1931 the "Delaware Canal," along with most of the other canals in Pennsylvania's vast system, ceased its commercial operations.

With the passage of the "canal era" most of the hundreds of miles of canals rapidly disappeared—their structures were either demolished to make room for industrial and commercial expansion or were left to deteriorate and crumble with the passage of time. Occasionally, on travels through Pennsylvania, remnants of some of these old canals can still be seen but, for the most part, they have become completely obliterated. In October 1940, the Commonwealth of Pennsylvania—realizing that all traces of this historically significant transportation system would soon be lost forever unless action at the state level was taken to protect and preserve some elements of it—acquired all the holdings along the entire length of the Delaware Canal. Since then the Pennsylvania Department of Forests and Waters has been operating and maintaining it as a State Park where boating, fishing, barge sight-seeing rides, picnicking, hiking and similar recreational pursuits are participated in by hundreds of thousands of visitors each year. Many of the communities along the Canal continue to use its waters for fire protection purposes as they have done ever since the Canal was constructed.

The Commonwealth of Pennsylvania is now engaged in a restoration program aimed at preserving, as nearly as possible, the authentic appearance of the Canal. Many of its original locks, aqueducts, bridges, and control structures built of stone masonry, timber and hand-wrought iron almost 140 years ago are still standing today—a tribute to the craftsmanship of the men who built them. These structures and the Canal itself can be, and are being, restored, rebuilt, and maintained as visual evidence of this bygone age; but the stories, legends and historical details of the old canal days can only be preserved in books such as Robert J. McClellan's *The Delaware Canal: A Picture Story*. The author has delved deeply into the history of the Delaware Canal and, by skillful use of both words and illustrations, has captured for posterity much of the flavor of the canal days of long ago.

MAURICE K. GODDARD
Secretary, Department of Forests
    and Waters
Commonwealth of Pennsylvania

To the hardy souls who worked and en-
dured the rugged life on this waterway; and
to those dedicated people who have done, and
are now doing, their part in maintaining the
Delaware Canal as a historic shrine.

Author's Note

The Delaware Canal: a Picture Story began one day—although I didn't realize it for some time—when the last thing on my mind was writing a book. I am a painter, not a writer.

A conversation with Frank Scheetz, an official of the Hunterdon County Bank in Lambertville, New Jersey, set me off down byways and waterways. Frank's hobby is photography, and his collection of local scenes had built up to fair size. His one desire in his later years, he told me, was to have a series of paintings made that would depict the old Canal in its bygone glory, using his photographs as source material.

This was a challenge which I accepted gladly. I agreed with Frank that the vanishing scene as it appeared about the turn of the century should be preserved, and that such a series might even be useful for further restoration of the Canal. I felt confident that my file of sketches made over the nearly two decades I had lived in New Hope, plus the photographs, would provide all that was necessary to present in pictures alone an accurate story, showing how the Canal and its barges had given this valley its place of importance in America's industrial growth.

But almost as soon as my work was started, I found that sources were sadly lacking. Points had to be checked as they kept cropping up. Days went by down in the dry bed of the Canal, drained for repairs, to make certain that the mechanism of a lock, for instance, actually did work as I had drawn it; endless time was spent in the archives at Harrisburg poring over old documents, or in libraries and museums; and countless hours passed in correspondence over an elusive fact. But in spite of all my efforts, there was still something lacking.

Finally I thought of seeking out the surviving men and women who had spent most of their lives in the service of the Delaware Canal. They still live on the banks of the Canal they love or not very far away—people bearing the old names of Dillon, Eichlen, Geddes, Henry, Kerrigan, Lear, Mason, McEntee, Miller, Reigel, Ruggles, Samsel, Sheets, Sigafoos, Snyder, Taylor, Warford, White, Winters, Yerkes, and others.

The New Hope railroad station as it appeared about the turn of the century.

These canallers are a special breed, many of them of Scotch-Irish descent, but occasionally of Pennsylvania "Dutch" and other backgrounds, and they are rugged, outspoken and industrious people. Though their ages range from the late seventies up into the nineties, they were in excellent health at the time I visited with them, a living testimonial to the values of the outdoor life and hard physical work. Try to outgrip one of them—their muscles are like steel.

These old timers made the gathering of material a joyous experience, giving of their time unstintingly, filling in gaps, and correcting misinformation. After talking with these men and women, with their keen memories and active minds, I realized that pictures alone would never capture the flavor of life on the Canal. I hadn't reckoned with the stories they told me. It might be impossible to reproduce the zestful delight and robust humor of the storytellers, but an attempt would have to be made.

At this point, willy-nilly, I became an author, taking notes at innumerable meetings and putting them into shape when I got home.

A few of the younger generation, descendants of the old bargemen and lock keepers, are still in the vicinity, and they were also generous with their recollections. They had begun life in this century on the Canal, but at the Canal's closing they were forced to find different means of livelihood. They speak of their childhood days nostalgically, telling of riding the boats with their fathers, walking with the mules, helping to steer, to tend locks, or working on maintenance crews.

Time was not governed as strictly by the clock as it is now, and there was more of it, or so it seems looking back. While the mules, who could have found their way blindfolded from Easton to Bristol, round trip, plodded the long stretches of the towpath, the bargeman sitting by the tiller regaled his children with funny and sometimes hair-raising stories. Without doubt many of these yarns were fancifully embroidered over the years, but that has always been the sailor's prerogative. Only an unimaginative stick-in-the-mud would have it otherwise.

Throughout this book I have set down old tales just as they were related to me. Some tell of practical jokes and their consequences; others sound like folklore; but whatever their content, they reflect the earthy and good-natured character of these born storytellers. May they give the reader much of the pleasure they gave me when I heard them directly! I can hear the old timer's voice as it trails off, "Well, sir, here's how things were on the Canal when I boated . . . ." To both the oldsters and the youngsters I am deeply indebted.

My place on the Towpath is practically an island. The Delaware River flows along at my back yard, the Canal at my front yard, and the feeder with its ever-humming waterfall on the south side. For a considerable time after it was no longer needed by the lock tenders, no one had any interest in owning the small stuccoed house, but it charmed me in its beautiful setting and I bought it, and used it at first as a studio and art school. Enlarged and remodeled over the years, it is now my home, where I am not far away from my old friends whose reminiscences take me back to the golden days of their Canal.

Robert J. McClellan

New Hope, Pennsylvania
April, 1967

Acknowledgment

Mr. and Mrs. Hal H. Clark of Doylestown have contributed immeasurably to historic preservation in the Delaware Valley, both by their efforts in behalf of the restoration and maintenance of historic landmarks, including the Canal itself, and by collecting and promulgating historical information that might otherwise have been lost. Articles written by Mrs. Clark have been most helpful to the author in the preparation of the text of this book.

Mr. Clark has served for eleven years as president of the Delaware Valley Preservation Society, and both he and Mrs. Clark are active in the Bucks County Historical Society. It is indeed fitting that the reconstructed wing dams in the Delaware River above New Hope will be named in honor of Mr. Clark.

R. J. McC.

Contents

The Delaware Canal

A Picture Story

·1·

The Coming of the Canal

This historic old waterway now known as the Delaware Canal was once called the Delaware Branch, or Delaware Division, Canal. From its start at Easton, Pennsylvania, at the slack-water pool formed by the Lehigh River Dam, the Canal runs sixty miles in a southeasterly direction on the Pennsylvania side of the Delaware River. It parallels the river through a small part of Northampton County and about fifty-two miles of Bucks County, then turns sharply inland to avoid the treacherous Trenton Falls. It continues almost due south to its outlet at Bristol Basin, which was the head of navigation for the tidal lower Delaware at the time the Canal was built, and only a few miles above the port of Philadelphia.

Since earliest times, long before there were canals or roads, the Delaware River was an artery for travel and trade. The Indians and the early European explorers and settlers used canoes, portaging around the falls and rapids. But the first large-scale transportation was by raft, which began early in the eighteenth century.

Rafting was possible only during spring freshets or an occasional high-water period at other times in the year, and then only downstream. It was a hazardous business. One old timer, Harry Warford, said, "Son, you probably don't know this about rafts. They were before your day. It took a dang good man to take a raft through the rapids. Once she got started downstream there was no stopping her in the current. That gave the rafts right-of-way over barges crossing the river and sometimes there were feuds between the raftsmen and the bargemen.

"You wouldn't remember that old covered bridge that crossed the Delaware before it was damaged in the early nineteen hundreds, either, would you? The raftsmen always guided their loads of lumber through the opening at Wells Falls [New Hope] by pulling the raft in line with the second window in the bridge from the Lambertville side, and heading her towards Bowman's Hill. When the flood took out this section in 1903, it more than just damaged the bridge—it also played heck with the raftsman's guiding point. The first man down after this catastrophe couldn't quite remember where the window had been, so he steered his raft by guess and by golly.

"Yep, you guessed it—he was off his mark by several feet and crashed into the wall of the wing dam. His load of timber loosened, going every which way, but mostly downstream—and into the water went the crew. Nobody was drowned, but when that raftsman finally surfaced and found a place to crawl up on, he was plenty mad.

"He cursed everything on both sides of the river, including the Union Mill at New Hope, the bridge, the barges, and everything else, not overlooking the human race."

Still, the rafts carried lumber, coal, flour from the gristmills (also dependent on the river for waterpower), and whiskey. As commerce increased, so did the growth of villages along the banks of the Delaware and its tributaries in Pennsylvania and New Jersey. Interest in finding new and better means of water transportation grew accordingly.

Boxlike "arks" came into use on the river about 1816, and for some years the Lehigh Coal and Navigation Company used these for descending navigation on the Lehigh River, loaded with anthracite bound for Philadelphia. When water was low in certain parts of the Lehigh, artificial freshets were created by movable dams. But at Easton the arks had to enter the upper Delaware, and go on down the river—a risky trip—to their destination, where, cargoes discharged, the vessels were broken up and sold for lumber.

A much more useful cargo carrier, designed some time before 1750, was the Durham boat. Two miles below the Durham blast furnace and forges, the site of the present village of Durham, Robert Durham constructed the first of these boats. It was specially designed for the current, navigating the rapids and carrying a heavy cargo. Since this was the only type of boat capable of making both the downstream trip to Philadelphia and the trip back upstream (with needed supplies) it stimulated the development of the river communities and their industries. It was guided downstream by a pair of eighteen-foot steering oars. Upstream it was propelled by setting poles heavily shod with iron and from twelve to eighteen feet long.

The Durham boat became more and more popular through the early decades of the nineteenth century and continued in use until the eighteen-sixties. But the practical politicians as well as the businessmen began to think of the advantages of connecting Delaware River traffic with that of other waterways, mainly the Susquehanna and Schuylkill Rivers. They were well aware that the Lehigh would soon have ascending navigation; that New Jersey was working on two canals, the Morris Canal and the Delaware and Raritan Canal, each one extending across the state from the Delaware River with access to New York Harbor and world shipping; and, finally, that if Pennsylvania built a canal from Easton to Philadelphia the Upper Delaware Valley would take its rightful place in the country's industrial growth. The planners intended to make the Canal the final link in a chain stretching from the inland coal regions far west and south, and east, through New Jersey, all the way to Europe.

The idea of canals was not new in America. William Penn had been familiar with the network of canals in his native England, and long before Washington was born, dreamed of them for his extensive properties in the future states of Pennsylvania, New Jersey, and Delaware. Washington foresaw political unity and economic independence for the new nation through canals. But craftsmen, materials, and—most important—credit were lacking, and he, too, died before his idea became a reality. True, there had been some small beginnings, short canals, supported by private capital, but not until 1825 was the first great commercial canal finished. It was the Erie, 350 miles long and entirely within New York State, from the Hudson River at Albany to the Great Lake for which it was named.

Ocean-going vessels sailed up the Hudson carrying thousands of tons of goods and streams of immigrants. Material and human cargoes were transferred at Albany to the Erie Canal where they moved out to the western frontier, creating industry and towns along the way. Commercial success was assured from the beginning.

"Canal fever" had been spreading all over the United States since 1815, when the War of 1812 ended. During the war, the British had successfully blockaded the coast and shipping had been virtually halted. Inland waterways would have given mobility to troops and materials as they later did so effectively during the Civil War, when barges and thousands of miles of canals played an important part. However, it was not national interest, but state interest and visions of personal wealth that motivated most of the promoters of the canals.

The building of the Erie, which started in 1817, and by-passed Pennsyl-

6

vania entirely, was the electrifying prod to Pennsylvanians, who felt threatened with financial ruin. The Port of Philadelphia, formerly second only to New York, was losing trade. Pennsylvanians wanted their share of the riches in the revolutions of transportation and industry.

By 1823 the clamor was so insistent that the General Assembly, under Governor John Andrew Shulze, passed an act appointing Canal Commissioners. The Pennsylvania Canal was authorized early in 1826 and its Delaware Division the following year. The Delaware Division was to have no direct connec-

The power wheels that were in the Delaware River alongside the Union Mill at New Hope. The outside wheel, right, had paddles which were turned by the flow of water, and it turned the inside wheel which was fastened to it by a center bar and couplings. The inside wheel caught the water in trough-like buckets and emptied it into a sluiceway under the mill and into the Canal on the other side. This helped keep up the water level in the Canal area below New Hope for barge operation. All that is now left of this installation are the stone walls that held the wheels in place.

tion with any other state-owned canal, but would supplement the independently financed Lehigh Canal about to be built. The Pennsylvania canal system was therefore conceived as three canals: There was the Schuylkill Canal, one up the Lehigh Valley (Lehigh Canal), and the third (the one with which this book is mainly concerned) south along the western bank of the Delaware down to tidewater at Bristol, a few miles from Philadelphia (Delaware Division).

The Pennsylvania Canal, which was to become the longest canal system in the country, was the first public utility voted by a government body to use public funds. This canal system did not consist entirely of waterways, as it carried cargoes overland in some places.

In 1827, the Lehigh Coal and Navigation Company hired Canvass White, the civil engineer who had been in charge of the eastern section of the Erie, as chief engineer for the Lehigh Canal. Josiah White (no relation to Canvass), a pioneer self-taught engineer and part owner of the company, had many suggestions. From boyhood days he had experimented and succeeded in canalizing

CROSS SECTION OF
DELAWARE CANAL

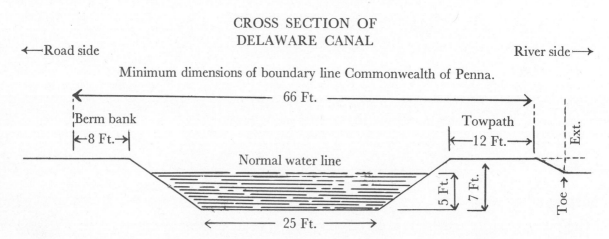

Normal water level was usually five feet in bank areas along this hand-dug channel. In some places it was slightly deeper. Within the lock areas, depths would be considerably more. Extension mark on towpath side shows where boundary line would extend from toe to slope if towpath was elevated above original ground level. This also applied to berm side. *(Copied from District Engineer's drawing, May 9, 1960)*

streams and rivers. Looking ahead, he insisted that the locks should be big enough to accommodate barges larger than those then in use; that the canal be deep and wide; and that the river itself be used wherever practicable. He worked at capacity himself and expected the same of his workmen. He frequently waded waist deep in the river to check progress. Josiah White was not one to compromise on quality in material or workmanship—or anything else for that matter—which did not endear him to some of his less ethically-minded rivals.

Wicket gates at feeder entrance in New Hope, showing rack bars, wicket bars or rods, and wicket openings at bottom of gate.

Naturally, Josiah White was vitally concerned with the work on the adjacent Delaware Canal. The canal commissioners voted to dig a canal parallel to the river. White wanted to canalize the Delaware itself, using the "bear trap" locks that he had invented and installed in the Lehigh River. These locks depended on hydrostatic pressure rather than muscle for operation. When they were first being installed, White had pledged his men to secrecy and when observers asked questions, the answer was "building bear traps." This satisfied the curious, as bears were common at that time. The secret was well kept until White was satisfied that he had invented the best possible locks for the purpose.

White argued that since the river provided a built-in water supply, why dig another? But other opinions prevailed, and only a few months after the Lehigh Canal was begun, digging started on the Delaware Canal. Work began at Bristol, the lower end, and up to New Hope a good schedule was maintained. The land was fairly level and not so rocky as might have been expected. The cost for labor and material was $12,000 a mile.

Canals of this period were pickax, shovel, and wheelbarrow operations. Teams of horses and mules, whenever available, pulled crude wooden scrapers, and heavy loads of rock and dirt. But mainly it was the brawn of the Irish immigrant that supplied the implements with power. Denied an education in the old country, from 1816 on they swarmed eagerly to the New World to become, at first, day laborers. They worked from sunrise to sunset, six days a week. A pick-and-shovel man was paid $1.00 a day, part in cash, part in whiskey. But all was not ditch digging: tree stump removal at 25¢ a stump could bring a superman from $5.00 to $12.00 a day. The more skilled built the locks, lockhouses and other buildings for the future operators of the Canal. They also constructed bridges and aqueducts—those fascinating troughs which carried the canal itself and its barges over depressions in the landscape. Sunday was the time to indulge in favorite avocations—eating and fighting.

Under proper supervision and strict discipline, the immigrants were hard workers, enduring bad housing, bad food, and long hours. When the "sickly

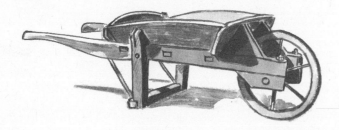

Side view of an aqueduct showing steel framework supported on both sides of the creek by cement foundations. The water of the Canal passes over the creek through the section within the framework. There are nine aqueducts on the Delaware Canal.

season" came, July through September, Asiatic cholera came with it. There was no cure, and many died. But there were always replacements as the work pushed ahead.

On December 7, 1830, over a year after the Lehigh Canal was ready, the first canal boat left New Hope with much fanfare. Four hours later it reached Bristol, twenty-five miles distant. But the Canal would not hold a sufficient amount of water and repairs had to be made. Provision had not been made for an adequate water supply; careless workmanship and shoddy materials caused leakage. Josiah White, who had counted on a connection with his Lehigh Canal,

11

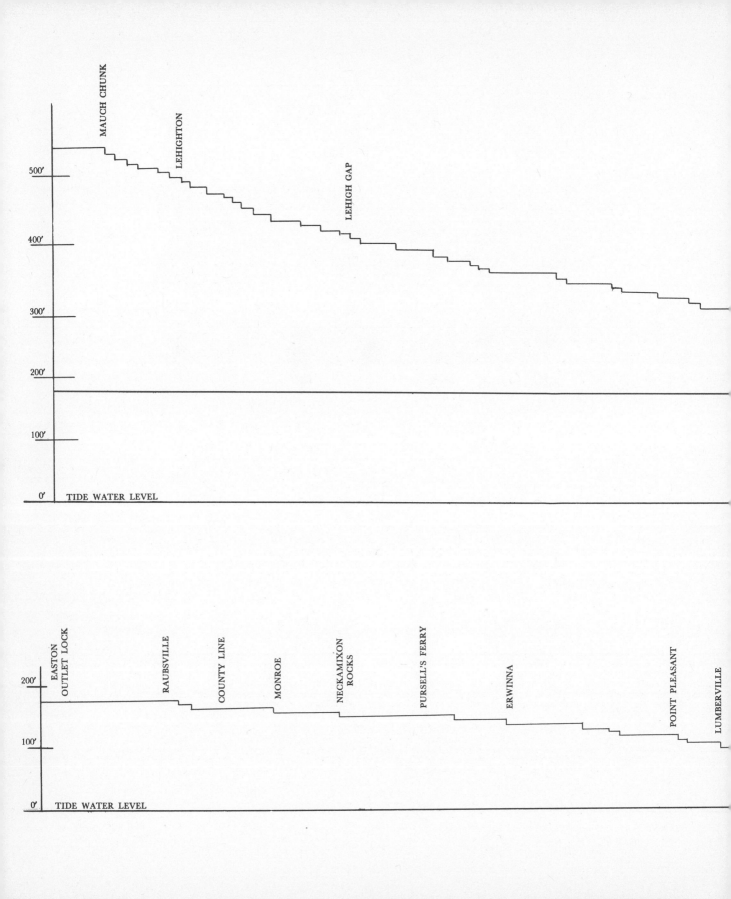

MAUCH CHUNK

LEHIGHTON

LEHIGH GAP

500'

400'

300'

200'

100'

0'   TIDE WATER LEVEL

EASTON
OUTLET LOCK

RAUBSVILLE

COUNTY LINE

MONROE

NECKAMIXON
ROCKS

PURSELL'S FERRY

ERWINNA

POINT PLEASANT

LUMBERVILLE

200'

100'

0'   TIDE WATER LEVEL

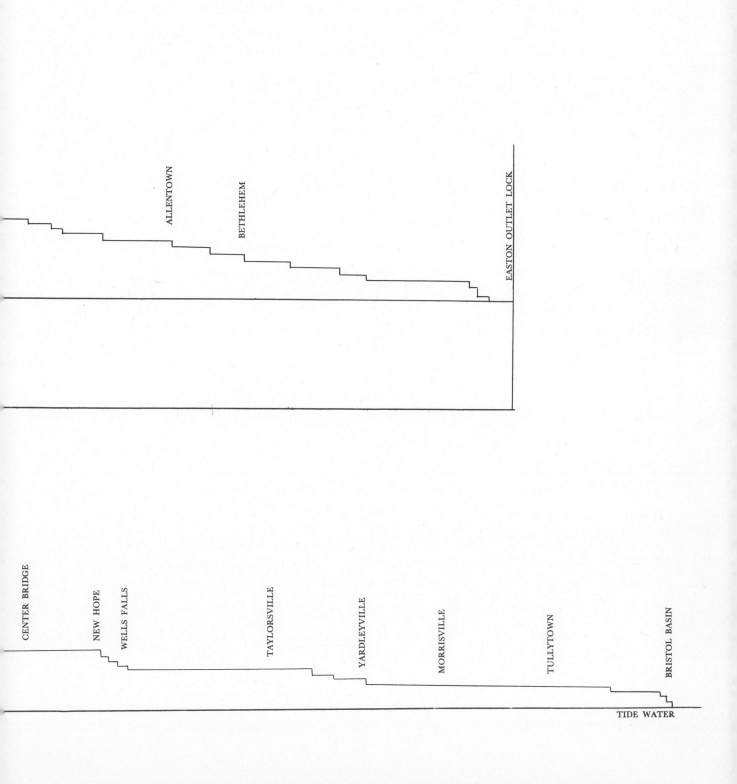

ALLENTOWN

BETHLEHEM

EASTON OUTLET LOCK

CENTER BRIDGE

NEW HOPE

WELLS FALLS

TAYLORSVILLE

YARDLEYVILLE

MORRISVILLE

TULLYTOWN

BRISTOL BASIN

TIDE WATER

was bitterly disappointed. The depth was also lacking for barge draft. This was corrected by raising the height of the banks by thirty inches.

The first two sections from Bristol to New Hope were not opened to commercial traffic until 1831. Finally, in September 1832, the Canal was opened throughout its entire length. Meanwhile, Josiah White had accepted the appointment as Pennsylvania's Canal Commissioner.

Feeders from streams, dams, and sluiceways were constructed, and a connection made with the Lehigh Canal, which, with other sources, assured enough water. A feeder is a branch transportation line, and bears the same relation to a canal as a spur does to a railway. A waterwheel-powered pump was added later at the wing dam at New Hope, where the water level was difficult to maintain, to raise water from the river into the Canal.

In 1840, outlet locks were built on opposite sides of the Delaware River, one in New Hope at the Delaware Canal and the other in Lambertville, New

Jersey, near the feeder to the Raritan Canal. A cable hookup ferried barges across the river, which cut off considerable mileage to Trenton, New Brunswick, and New York. Barges could then go back up the Delaware River to Bordentown and across New Jersey to New York City, by way of the Raritan Canal. Under Josiah White the Canal flourished, and it continued for almost one hundred years as a very important utility in the East.

The greatest traffic years on the Canal were those just before the Civil War, when annually more than one million tons of coal alone were carried, as

Ring rock at New Hope used for helping pull
boats and rafts over the rapids.

well as thousands of tons of other commodities—pig iron, stone, paper, ore,
lumber, liquor, lime, and grains and other food supplies. There is a story that
there was one other cargo—bargemen who carried goods to New York would
sometimes make a little money on the side bottling Canal water and selling it
to the city slickers as spring water.

When the Canal was at its peak of operation between 2500 and 3000
barges were in use and as many as one hundred at a time were tied up in the
Bristol Basin waiting to be towed to their destinations. The Red Line used a
bulls eye insignia—red center, white circle—which was known as "the fried
egg." The Bernard and Samsel Line, the last one to run barges on the Canal,
gave their boats such names as *I. M. Church, W. A. Lysering,* and *Capt. Alex-
ander Bartholomew.* There were also some private owners, among them one
Michael Uhler, the founder of Uhlerstown, Pennsylvania, who had among his
other interests coal yards, lime kilns, a country store and the job of postmaster.

As the railroad line burgeoned and began to compete for freight, traffic on
the Canal declined. It had been operated much as the turnpikes are today, by
the Canal Commission. In 1858, when the returns to the state had considerably
diminished, the Canal was sold to private operators. The last paying barge
passed in December, 1931, and in that year the Canal ceased operation and

reverted to state control. The Delaware Division was set aside in 1940 as Theodore Roosevelt State Park. As time passed, public interest in the Canal increased. The Delaware Valley Protective Association, with the help of other organizations and individuals, brought about its restoration.

When the Canal was closed to commercial traffic, the adjoining land and houses that had been constructed for employees were offered to them at very reasonable prices, possibly as a gesture of appreciation for the loyal services they had rendered over the years. Many, of course, took advantage of this opportunity. Some did not, and the remaining properties were sold to private bidders. This is how I acquired my house on the Canal, which at first I used as a studio and art school.

In the later days of the Canal, while it was still in full operation, motor-powered boats came into use and they were permitted to pass in and out. When the State took over maintenance and supervision of the Canal, all motorized units were forbidden use of the Canal, and numerous other restrictions were imposed.

I was unaware of these rules and restrictions, and decided to construct a boat landing within the feeder area. It took me nearly a week to complete the job, using a lot of good lumber and many heavy rocks. It was solid, I thought, as the Rock of Gibraltar. Shortly after the job was finished, I stood admiring my handiwork. Russ Paetzel, the superintendent of the Canal, happened to come along. He informed me that I might have to tear down my boat landing, but added, "I'll check with Harrisburg and see if they will let you keep it for personal use only."

I went home to Doylestown that night trying to think of some strategy to save my landing. Next morning I returned to the Canal and walked down to the feeder to take an admiring look at my "Rock of Gibraltar." It was gone! I couldn't believe my eyes; not a stone nor a single piece of wood gave evidence that anything had ever been constructed on this spot.

Finally a neighbor, seeing me standing and staring at nothing, stopped to tell me what had happened. Heavy rains had caused a spot flood the night before, missing my place by a few feet. It took everything in its path, damaging the collector's office below me and the River House below that. Russ appeared very sympathetic, but I think he was chuckling to himself about my "Rock of Gibraltar."

Two factors not considered at all in the Canal's planning are the most important in its restoration and revitalization—its beauty and its historical importance. Thousands of visitors flock each year to the area to enjoy the natural beauty of the surroundings and visit the many landmarks.

No lovelier setting could have been chosen. The Upper Delaware is separated from the Lower by a natural barrier, the Trenton Falls, a rocky channel with a drop of ten feet in less than three-quarters of a mile. Though perilous to shipping (only the remarkable Durham boats could make the ascent) the Upper Delaware is spectacular for its very faults, white water over boulders

The Canal water flows through an aqueduct which is built over a stream, with a footbridge for the mules.

Barge about to pass over stream, which flows under the aqueduct between stone walls. The aqueduct itself is made of wood, usually yellow pine or white oak. The wood never rotted as long as water covered it.

The underside structure of the aqueduct.

Dry bed view of aqueduct and walking bridge.

and many waterfalls. The area where the Canal began, verdant with pines, hemlocks, hardwoods, and stands of flowering rhododendrons, dogwood, and laurel, gradually gives way to the rolling hills of a gentle pastoral scene, where often still stand white painted or fieldstone houses, red barns, springhouses for keeping meat and dairy products fresh, and rich cultivated fields.

The visitor to these areas of quiet beauty can only try to recreate in his mind's eye the Canal full of barges waiting their turn to pass through the locks, the now abandoned towpaths populated by mules, the air filled with the sounds of boat horns, harness bells, and conch horns. It is such a re-creation which the author hopes to aid and foster in this book.

· 2 ·

A Trip on the Canal

Having become acquainted with the general background of the development of the canal system, one might best gain an understanding of its actual workings by taking an imaginary barge run down the waterway. Let's say we will start at Easton and head towards Bristol. Our ultimate destination may be Philadelphia or New York Harbor. We will suppose conditions to be as they were around the turn of the century, when the Canal was still in full operation.

Our barge is loaded in the Lehigh-Easton area. It is eighty-seven feet in length, ten feet six inches wide, and eight feet high. Once loaded with coal, one of the most common cargoes, it rides about two feet above water. Two types of barges were used in this canal system. One, called the stiff type, was built in one section. Its draft (the depth of water the boat displaces) was greater and its maneuverability limited. This was later replaced by the "squeezer" type, which was built in two sections and could be used in numerous ways. Its out-

21

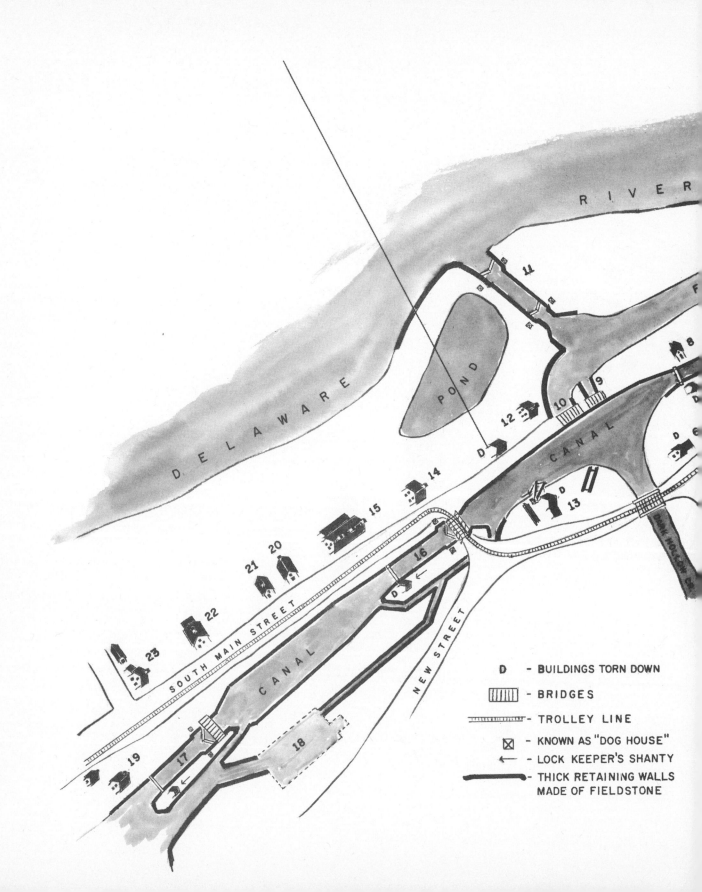

R I V E R

DELAWARE

POND

CANAL

11

8

9

10

12

D

14

15

13

D

16

20

21

22

23

SOUTH MAIN STREET

CANAL

NEW STREET

19

17

18

DARK HOLLOW DR.

D — BUILDINGS TORN DOWN

⬛ — BRIDGES

▦ — TROLLEY LINE

☒ — KNOWN AS "DOG HOUSE"

← — LOCK KEEPER'S SHANTY

▬ — THICK RETAINING WALLS MADE OF FIELDSTONE

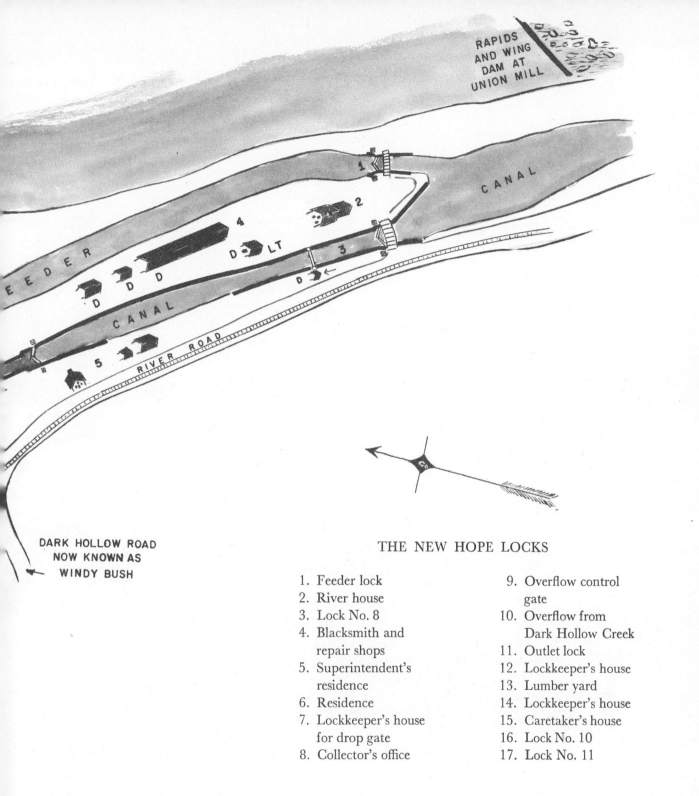

RAPIDS
AND WING
DAM AT
UNION MILL

CANAL

FEEDER CANAL

RIVER ROAD

DARK HOLLOW ROAD
NOW KNOWN AS
WINDY BUSH

THE NEW HOPE LOCKS

1. Feeder lock
2. River house
3. Lock No. 8
4. Blacksmith and repair shops
5. Superintendent's residence
6. Residence
7. Lockkeeper's house for drop gate
8. Collector's office
9. Overflow control gate
10. Overflow from Dark Hollow Creek
11. Outlet lock
12. Lockkeeper's house
13. Lumber yard
14. Lockkeeper's house
15. Caretaker's house
16. Lock No. 10
17. Lock No. 11

Three styles of barges used on the Delaware Division and other canals. The upper two are the "stiff" type. Below is the "squeezer," found to be the most practical for use on the Delaware Canal. This one was operated by Levi Winters.

standing feature was its double-section construction. Each half was sealed as a separate boat. These "halves" were fastened together with hooks and the two sections were drawn close. A bolt fitted in the couplings held the sections together. By moving a large iron handle one way or the other, a bolt could be slipped in or out of the couplings on the other half; thus either bolt held the two sections together or allowed them to be separated. If the barge had to turn in the Canal, or a part of it had to be moved into a narrow passage, the bolt was pulled and each unit moved separately. This gave the boat considerably more maneuverability than the stiff type had, and saved manpower and time when repairs were needed. The two-section construction also permitted carrying two different cargoes—a perishable item in one section, perhaps, and coal in the other.

Our imaginary barge will be pulled by a team of mules. When one old-timer was asked the inevitable question of why mules were used rather than horses, he answered, "Well, I'll tell you—fer one thing they're a mite easier to handle than a horse. They don't get excited easy and they ain't very fond of water. Now you take a horse, if he gets dry or hot he's apt to take off and head straight for the water in the Canal, and let me tell you, sir, gettin' a horse out of the Canal ain't easy."

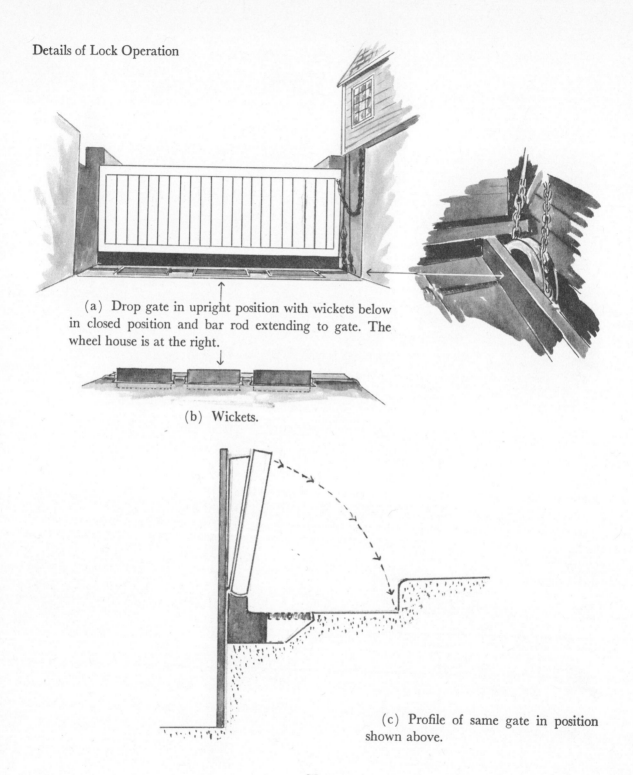

(a) Drop gate in upright position with wickets below in closed position and bar rod extending to gate. The wheel house is at the right.

(b) Wickets.

(c) Profile of same gate in position shown above.

(d) The chain fastened to the fall gate is wound around a spool-type gear as it tightened or released its hold on the gate.

(e) A wicket wheel is fastened to the shaft of the gear wheel by a coggle bolt. Both wheels, one in the house, the other in the water, needed only a half turn to open or close wickets.

(f) Fall gate about to drop to flat position for passing of a barge.

(g) Wickets open and water rushing through.

HINGE BOAT IN TWO SECTIONS

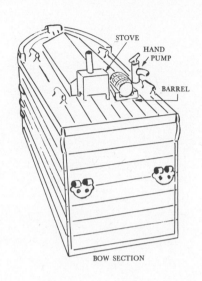

BOW SECTION

STOVE

HAND PUMP

BARREL

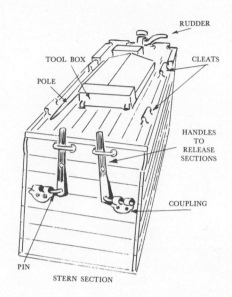

RUDDER

TOOL BOX

CLEATS

POLE

HANDLES TO RELEASE SECTIONS

COUPLING

PIN

STERN SECTION

LOOKING FACE DOWN ON THE BARGE
87½ FT. LONG

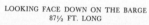

TOP DECK COVER FOR CARGO SPACE

NIGHT-HAWKER

STOVE   BARREL   TOOL BOX

HINGES

HATCHWAY

CABIN AREA

RUDDER

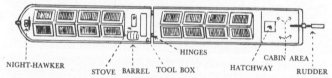

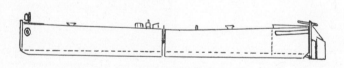

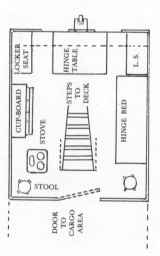

LOCKER SEAT

CUP-BOARD

STOVE

HINGE TABLE

STEPS TO DECK

L. S.

HINGE BED

STOOL

DOOR TO CARGO AREA

APPROXIMATE CABIN SIZE: 12 FT. LONG, 10 FT. WIDE, 7 FT. HIGH

28

Probably two mules will pull our barge, although sometimes as many as four or five were used. This depended on the number of barges and cargo. Generally, each operator owned his own team and he hired out himself and his team to someone who owned a fleet of barges.

With bells a-tingling, our barge starts out. The first lock it passes through after leaving the loading station on the Lehigh is called the weigh lock and is just wide enough for one barge. After the barge is secured within the lock, all the water is let out, allowing the barge to rest on a huge scale device. A house close to the lock wall maintains weighing gear. The captain of the barge is issued a slip showing the weight of the load, time, and charges. Duplicate records are filed in the office of the weigh lock. Our barge probably weighs some ninety-odd tons, the average weight of a loaded barge. Since it cost a little over half a cent per ton for a company to ship coal, shipping by barge was extremely inexpensive and one of the main reasons for the Canal's existence.

We now start our journey in earnest. The Canal had to be constructed so that at all points there would be minimum depth to allow for the draft of the barges. Since the altitude of the land drops from over five hundred feet at Coalport to zero at Bristol where the level meets tidewater, a series of locks was constructed. A lock, simply defined, is an enclosure in the Canal with gates at each end, used to raise or lower the barge (depending on whether it is going upstream or downstream) from level to level. Once a barge is within a lock, the water level is adjusted, through manipulation of the gates, to the next level and then the boat proceeds. On this journey, we will pass through locks numbered 24 through 12 before reaching 11 to 8 in the New Hope area. (The workings of the New Hope locks will be described in detail.)

Throughout our trip, both within the lock areas and the long open stretches, the water level is maintained by lock gates, fall gates, control gates, and sluiceways.

In the Delaware Division, locks have a drop of approximately five to

Lock tender turns the handle that opens wickets. Fall gate coupling and part of the old stove can be seen at left.

twenty-one feet. This was worked out in detail by engineers who determined where the locks should be placed. Other factors they had to consider were the time it would take to pass through a lock, the amount of water needed to maintain sufficient depth to float the barge, evaporation, filtration, and leakage.

Along the open stretches of the waterway, the Canal banks are nothing more than soil, with grass and plants as a binder. One side is called the berm bank, and the other the towpath—the side next to the river, used by the men and mules in shuttling barges up and down the Canal.

Within the lock areas, the sides are built up with field stone; sometimes ties and planking were used to form the sidewalls. This allows boats to pull in close for loading and letting other boats pass. It also prevents mud and plant life from jamming or binding lock gate operation. Ties were crossed-hatched and securely set on the bottom of the lock enclosures.

After coming out of the weighing lock, the first community of any size we pass is Riegelsville. Here is a coal yard and dock as well as W. Walters' saloon, which probably makes this community a favorite stopping place for the boatman. Here he can mix business with beer and grog. About a mile below Riegelsville is the Durham Furnace Works. This is a little community in itself made up of dwellings and shop buildings. Durham Creek feeds into the Canal at this point, but the Canal has its own feeder that connects with the loading depot and shops. Next comes Kitnersville; many of the Canal workers live in and around this town. Uhlerstown follows. It has lime kilns, a boat yard and a number of shops. Upper Black Eddy, though not as thickly populated as some of the other communities, has two hotels.

As our barge continues, it will probably meet a boat coming in the opposite direction. We may pass the other barge in either a friendly or an unfriendly manner. In the more amicable situation, when they come parallel, neither bargeman has to disengage his line from the team, providing both boats are not carrying too much cargo and are high on the water. One simply lifts his line over and the other bargeman works his line under. When hostile bargemen pass, the one who has to yield the right of way, by stated Canal regulations, unhooks his line from the team and either tosses it to his helper on the boat or, if the oncoming barge is not drawing too much draft, holds the line and lets it lie slack in the water so it can be passed over. The one unhooking loses some time, which wouldn't improve the already strained relations between these particular bargemen. Competition was keen among bargemen, and if, in the course of a week, one boated more loads than his competitor, it was something to brag about.

A former canal boat man recently described the experience at a meeting of the Bucks County Historical Society. He was about fourteen, and was helping his father operate his barge, shipping coal. Starting out in the morning with an empty barge, they would head for the loading depot. His father always used three mules; most of the others used two. On this morning they spotted a competitor, with whom they were not on friendly terms, about a quarter of a mile ahead. "Son," said the bargeman, "you git on this rudder and keep 'er straight. I'm gonna git these mules a-movin' and we'll pass Jake before he gits to the lock."

Lock above Upper Black Eddy. Sluiceway with control gate
is on the left, drop gate in upright position, and wicket gate partly
open.

The lock operation took about twelve minutes in each passage, and the lock ahead was a single one, so the barge that got there first would gain about fifteen minutes. "Well, sir," said the old timer, "Pa whupped them critters up to a good trot and we overtook Jake and passed him about two hundred feet from the lock. We loaded our boat and on the way back met Jake, who was only halfway to the loading station. Pa never told me what Jake said to him when they passed, but I could see he was mad and glarin' awful hard."

Approximately two miles below Upper Black Eddy nestles a quiet and pleasant little village. It is Erwinna and even in today's changing world it retains much of its former charm and character, the large trees spreading their shade over the homes of families who have lived here for generations. A long stretch of Canal follows, broken only by an occasional barn or house and the lime quarry about halfway between Erwinna and Point Pleasant.

Point Pleasant is a busy little community — a maze of waterway, bridges, and roads. Lumberville, as its name would indicate, has as its main business a large sawmill and lumber yard. A covered bridge crosses the river at this point to Bools Island on the Jersey side. It is a toll bridge, as were all bridges of this period, and one of the most travelled crossings of the Delaware, for at Bools

Canal locks at Lumberville. On the "dog house" at left, a handle turns cogs that fit into a rack bar attached by couplings to the "dog house," and by an iron bar that runs through it to the gate itself. The heavy wheels on top of each gate control the gate's wickets. This is the only set of locks on the Delaware Canal with such an arrangement.

Island is an inlet to the feeder canal leading to the Raritan. Next we come to Center Bridge, where a covered bridge crosses the river to Stockton, New Jersey.

As barge approaches the wide-water section of New Hope, we find a good place to tie up for a brief rest before starting through the locks. The bargeman can walk down to the stores if he needs anything and at the foot of Ferry Street is a tavern where a dry and weary man can get a tot of rum or a pitcher of beer before returning to his duties.

Back in the barge, the boat is ready to start its journey through the four locks in the New Hope area. New Hope's locks are all double, although the single lock is more common throughout the system. Since double locks permit two boats to go through side by side, shifting from a double course to a single one causes bottlenecks on the Canal much as they do on the modern highway when a double lane turns into a one-lane road. In three parts of the New Hope area there are wide-water sections, which allow several barges at a time to move in and out, make changes or transfers, and tie up without interfering with the other bargeman's operation. Since it takes from twelve to fifteen minutes to pass through each lock operation, this is a help.

Our barge is now in the wide-water section just above Lock No. 11 and getting ready to enter. From here we can see a lumber yard where repair boats and work scows were kept and minor repairs on barges could be handled. Long wooden slides measuring eight feet by eight feet and fastened with bolts to abutments could be angled to water level and hold the boats while carpenters did the necessary work. Only small boats were repaired in this yard; if there was considerable work to be done the barges would be sent somewhere else, perhaps to the Uhlerstown boat yard. In the meantime, another boat would be sent down to replace the one taken away. A loading station is also located in the Lock No. 11 area.

When our bargeman wants to enter the lock he signals by a blast on the horn. The lock tender then closes the wickets on the wicket gate and goes up to

Drop gate in upright position, holding water back to the proper level and allowing only enough through the openings and over the top to supply the area below.

Within this small house are the wheels and mechanism for lowering and raising the drop gate and opening and closing the wickets.

The drop gate in upright position in winter when the Canal is dry.

open the wicket under the drop gate, and pulls the chain to start the momentum, releasing the water pressure against the gate. As the water gushes through the wickets, the heavy gate gradually eases down into the water to rest in the trough-like recess on the floor of the Canal, allowing the water level within the lock to rise. When the proper depth for the draft of the boat is reached, the lock tender signals the bargeman, who then starts his team of mules pulling the boat over the lowered drop gate into the lock. The wickets on the drop gate are immediately closed when the barge clears the gate. About eight turns on the wheel attached by a chain to the drop gate starts it on its ascent, and the water pressure completes the job of raising the gate up to the closed position, the barge within the lock.

The lower, or wicket, gate is now opened fully by means of the rack and shifted smoothly into a recess in the side wall. A barge traveling upstream would use the same procedure in reverse, the wicket gate being opened before the fall gate. Fall gates, also called drop gates, were always at the upstream end of a lock where the water pressure was constant. The wicket gate was at the downstream end. By means of the wickets at the bottom of both gates, the water flow could be controlled and the level raised or lowered.

Sluiceways parallel to the lock area and bypassing the lock itself connected the flow of water above the drop gate to the area below the wicket gate. If additional water was needed to raise the level for boats coming upstream, the sluiceways were fully opened, raising the boat to a height for entering the lock. The drop level at each particular lock had to be considered in adjusting the water level for a boat to pass over.

The mules pull the barge out into the next wide water area, where the barge master's signal has carried to all locks, and through Lock No. 10.

Flora K. Henry, a lockkeeper's daughter, born in 1911 and now a resident of Point Pleasant, Pennsylvania, remembers the angry blasts from one particular barge family, the Winters. "Those Winters! They were always ready for a

The barge tied up at Lock No. 10 could have been the one that Levi Winters, Sr., operated. The Winters' house is at left. At the right is a stack of lumber ready for loading.

A barge has just passed Lock No. 11 and the drop gate of Lock No. 10 has been lowered, allowing the needed water to enter. When the boat is inside the lock, the drop gate will be raised, locking in the barge. The wicket gate will then be opened and the barge will pass out of Lock No. 10.

A section of Lock No. 10 with Lock No. 11 in the distance. The drop gate is in upright position, holding back the water. The overflow at the drop gate is continuous and the water passes on through the open wicket gate. The trolley car crossed a wooden bridge at Lock No. 10, passing on over the Canal and continuing down River Road.

The wide water area below Lock No. 10. At left is a carpenter boat tied up at the lumber yard.

fight. We could always tell when they were on their way to pass through a lock. We didn't even have to see their boat when they started blowing. Dad would say, 'Here come the Winters.' Then he'd shove his pipe in his mouth and start getting things ready and wait for the fireworks. They sure got mad when you held them up. In a double lock operation, you see, it wouldn't pay to let one boat through at a time, if there was another boat close by, so we'd wait until another barge was ready to enter the lock and put them through together.

"Most barge operators didn't mind, but the Winters would stomp around, argue, and try to bull Dad into opening the gates. Dad would just sit there with his pipe in his mouth. Levi's face would get so red he'd almost have a stroke. He did die with high blood pressure, and only in his early fifties. John, the youngest brother, died not long after, with a similar condition. They sure were fighting Irish!"

Our barge is now approaching Lock No. 10. The drop gate has been lowered and wicket gate opened allowing the barge to continue its journey. The rise

40

Passing from Lock No. 10 into another wide water area. The two openings in the bank between the barn and the lock tender's house release water pressure when heavy rains bring too much water into the basin. The single opening at the right is the control level gate.

Lock No. 9 and the collector's office. Here the draft of the boat is measured to estimate its weight, destination recorded, and charges entered in the record book.

A close-up of the control level gate and the collector's office. Beyond are sheds and a general store.

The barge in a wide water area between Lock No. 10 and Lock No. 9. At left is the collector's office and at right the drop gate house. The large white house at the right is no longer standing, and other buildings have been changed to some extent.

and fall of the water level is not as great as one would think, when transfers from one level to another take place.

This system of lockage was a vast improvement over the earlier canal systems, which required great physical strength to manipulate the heavy door-like gate. By taking advantage of the hydrostatic pressure, one man was able to operate both upper and lower gates. Once the drop gate was closed and held in position by the water, pressure within a lock was negligible, and lower gate could be moved without difficulty.

At Lock No. 9, Harry Warford, who is in charge of the Toll House, wants to know our destination—is it the Bristol Basin or the Raritan Canal on the Jersey side? Since we are heading toward the Raritan Canal, he raises a red flag on a pole beside his shanty to signal the keepers on the east bank of the Dela-

PROFILE DRAWING OF LOCK NO. 9

Length within gate 98 feet.
Water levels are exaggerated
for better illustration.

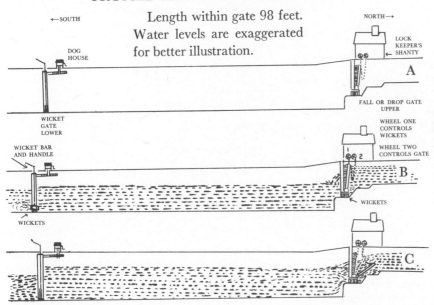

A. Lock in dry bed condition, and with upper and lower gates and all wickets closed.

B. The lock is now in normal use, with wickets on lower gate open, on upper gate closed, and water passing through slowly.

C. A signal from the bargeman's horn, as he approaches from the north, indicates his intention to pass through the lock. Wickets on the fall gate are opened and as the water pressure against it decreases it drops down, allowing the barge to pass over. The lockkeeper hurries down to the gate below and closes the wickets.

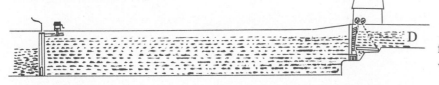

D. Lock No. 9 is now filled and the barge is within the two gates.

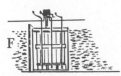

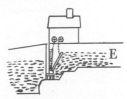

F. A "dog house" on each bank controls the opening of each wicket gate. Large handles are turned, drawing back the gate into a recess in the wall, allowing the barge to pass through without jamming the gates. When the barge is clear, the gates are closed, and once more the lock appears as in Illustration B.

E. Now the lockkeeper goes back to the fall gate and makes eight complete turns on the large wheel (No. 2) and closes wickets on this gate. Illustration shows angle of gate after eight turns. The water pressure against it does the rest, pushing the gate back to its normal position, locking the barge within the two gates.

North side of the wicket gate that opens into the feeder, showing the framework.

Top view of the wicket gate shows the bar extending through the heavy beams and timber bar that is attached to the gate by a swivel arrangement and fastened to a rack bar that enters the "dog house."

The barge on its way up the feeder approaching the outlet lock. The feeder runs parallel to Locks 9 and 8, but at a level with the river, which is several feet lower than the lock system. At the right is the rear of the collector's office.

As the barge approaches New Hope outlet lock it will pass both overflow control gate and overflow. Behind these is the lumber shed between Locks 10 and 9.

ware that a boat will soon be entering the feeder for the cable crossing. No signal flag is necessary for the journey down to the Bristol Basin. Both the freight charge and the separate charge for the river crossing are entered in the record book. The freight charge is determined by using the gauging stick to measure the draft and so judging the cargo weight.

Sometimes a bargeman, taking a load of coal down the Canal, would barter some of it for whiskey, eggs, butter, or vegetables along the way, or give a basket or two to a friend. This left him short at the weighing station, and he had a trick for covering his discrepancy. The barge had an air space several inches deep in the bottom, which caught the water used to wet down the coal. It was supposed to be kept dry by pumping out water as it leaked in. Just before com-

After leaving Lock No. 8 the barge passes through the entrance to the feeder lock.

An empty barge on its way to the loading station. Mules are feeding from baskets as they start the day's haul. The snapping turtle was a common sight along the Canal banks.

ing to the weighing station, the bargeman would pump water into this space to raise the draft and make it appear that he had the same hundred tons he started with.

At the sight of Harry Warford's red flag, two workers at the inlet lock on the New Jersey side immediately begin preparations. They throw ropes and other gear into a light flat-bottomed boat and start across the Delaware. Their sole responsibility is moving the barges by cable from one side of the river to the other. From long experience, they know the river thoroughly — speed of current, depth, and how the weather will affect it at the time of crossing.

At Lock No. 8, the last of the New Hope locks our barge will pass through, we go by a tavern, the River House, through the wicket gate, under a camelback bridge, into another wide-water section. Here we turn around and enter the feeder by way of a wicket gate.

The trip up the feeder is short; the inside gates of the outlet lock are already open. Inside the lock, the boat waits until preparations for the crossing are complete. Meanwhile, the mules are released from the hookup, and start back along the feeder with one driver; another stays with the barge. Driver and mules go

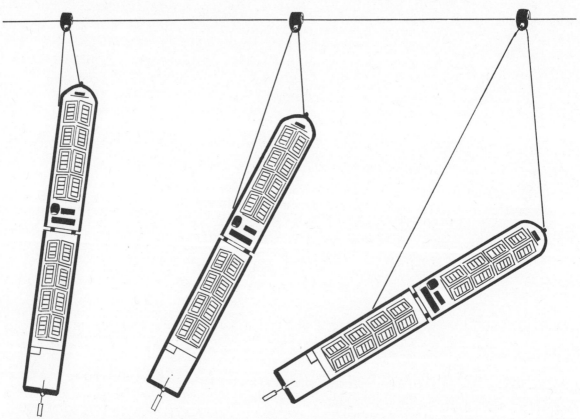

Pulley hook-up to barge with boat facing upstream. Angle would vary depending on the speed of the current. These angles are not necessarily accurate, but merely indicate the method.

As the barge enters the river, a rope fastened to it is tied to a winch. The two men at the right are tightening the rope by turning the winch, while the man on the front of the barge takes up the slack as the barge eases out on the pulley line hook-up. The man on the point is directing the operation.

back past the River House, the collector's office, then go up Main Street to the old covered bridge between New Hope and Lambertville, New Jersey. A fine sight they make clumping across the rattling boards, bells tinkling, harness jingling and the driver yelling "Gidyap, you lazy so-and-sos!"

The cable crossing procedure is similar to a ferry's except that it is entirely manual. A cable line tower stands several yards upstream from the outlet lock on each side of the river. Maneuvering the barge into the current requires great dexterity and precision. A rope is tied to the stern and attached to a winch, firmly planted on the upstream bank where the cable tower is located. The winch has a hole to accommodate a long-handled bar. As two men grasp the bar ends and run around and around at top speed, the rope tightens and draws the barge the rest of the way out of the lock into the eddy, which has been created by a half-submerged floating dock close to shore and just above the outlet lock. This breaks the strong current that would otherwise hit the barge and carry it out of control down the river.

The barge is pulled into the outlet lock. One set of gates has been opened to allow the boat to enter; the other set is kept closed to prevent water escaping into the river and lowering the water within the lock, which is needed to float the barge out into the river. The mules are straining at their traces to get the boat set within the lock. Two men are on their way over in a rowboat to take the barge across, and above is the three-inch cable that is attached to towers on both sides of the river.

At the outlet locks on both the Pennsylvania and New Jersey sides, where the feeder empties into the river, unloading scows were kept. If the river was low, it might be necessary to transfer some of the barge's load to a scow, to make the barge draw less water in crossing. The scow was towed alongside, or brought over later.

Now is the time for the hookup to angle for the crossing of the Delaware. One end of the line from the pulley on the cable is tied securely to the bow of the

The crossing. The barge is hooked to the cable at an angle for a slow current.

barge and the other end is hooked to the side along the gunwales. The rope is lengthened or shortened to give the necessary angle for the crossing. The slower the current, the greater the angle, so that in a fast-moving current, a barge would be headed almost straight upstream. A boat crossing too fast may jam and damage the outlet gates, causing delay and costly repairs. Expert workers sometimes find it more expedient to take a barge in backwards, and then turn it after it reaches the first open area beyond the gate section.

Now on the New Jersey side at Lambertville, our barge will be hooked up to the mules again, go on through the outlet locks to the Raritan feeder, proceed to the Raritan Canal, and head for New Brunswick. From there we will be towed to New York tide points.

A loaded barge is tied up on the Raritan Canal on the New Jersey side after the crossing. Below, a barge is being unloaded. Like most of the barges operating in the Delaware Division, this is a "squeezer," and the half which has been unloaded rides high in the water, taking very little draft. When the barges are emptied, they return to the outlet lock on the New Jersey side, cross back to Pennsylvania, and enter the Delaware Canal for the return trip.

The empty barge, drawing about fourteen inches of water, is about to leave the outlet lock of the Raritan Canal and be hooked up to the cable for its return to the Pennsylvania side. The rowboat tied to the stern will bring the two men back to their station on the New Jersey side. Partly visible outside the lock is an unloading scow.

Another way of reaching New York from our starting point at Easton would have been to enter the Morris Canal in New Jersey, which runs across the northern part of the state, ending at the Port of Newark. The Morris Canal had been leased to the Lehigh Valley Railroad in 1871, and was not abandoned until 1924.

Had our destination been Philadelphia, we would have continued on the Delaware Division to Bristol. Here was the famous "bump bridge," the only one of its kind on the Canal. The hinges on which the two sections of the bridge moved were counterbalanced so that when a boat bumped into it, the bridge opened, and it swung shut again when the barge had passed. At Bristol, we would have entered the Delaware River, lined up with about nineteen other other barges, and towed by one of three tugs to the Port of Philadelphia.

*   *   *

Many changes have come to the Canal over the years since our imaginary barge trip, but happily much of it is still the same. Lock No. 11 at New Hope is no longer in operation. Pete Pascuzzo's barge parties now start here for a round trip to a point beyond Center Bridge, a restful and picturesque journey with a cargo of people instead of merchandise. The former grist mill at New Hope is now the Bucks County Playhouse, and the feeder on the New Jersey side of the river, where boats used to enter the Delaware and Raritan Canal, has been blocked off.

The two hotels at Upper Black Eddy are long gone, but the old River House at New Hope, built in 1794 for the ferry trade, still flourishes under the name of Chez Odette. There is little left at Durham Furnace, and the lumber yards and boat yards no longer exist. But many of the old buildings along the Canal have been restored as residences or business establishments. Painters and photographers can still capture the beauty and serenity of bygone days. If a bargeman of a century ago could return and make one more run down the Canal, many sights would be strange to him, but he still would feel at home.

· 3 ·

Life on the Canal

The bargeman's life was unique. His boat was often his home — at least from April 1 to December 10, when the Canal was open for traffic. Many barges were family boats with husband, wife and children living aboard. All of them had cabins, about ten feet by nine feet, built in the stern. Their top surface was in line with the gunwales about ten inches above the deck, which allowed for windows on both sides. One entered by descending through the hatchway, which had a cover for bad weather, down a ladder-like set of stairs. In the cabin were all the essentials. Sleeping bunks and tables were hinged and could be dropped against the wall when not in use, leaving more floor space. A locker, an enclosed boxlike bench, housed necessities for preparing meals. Most important, perhaps, was the stove placed near the hatchway steps, which was used for heating and for cooking. The stove was called a "boatman's choice," since there was a variety of models among which to choose.

The womenfolk fixed up the cabins to make them as homelike as the limited space allowed; they had colorful curtains, fancy tablecloths, and gay oilcloth on the floor. Oil or kerosene lamps shed a warm glow, and pictures — usually cut from a calendar — decorated the walls.

Another stove, usually a rectangular model called the Franklin stove, was up on deck. It kept a pot of coffee hot and was handy for taking the chill from hands and feet. Also on deck would be a good-sized box with a sloping lid in which were stored tools, rope, pulleys and wedges. A wood barrel containing drinking water and a gallon jug of rum or whiskey were also on deck, along with various poles and hooks laid along the sides of the barge.

A   B   C

BOX STOVE   DRUM STOVE   WOODWARD STOVE

DRUM STOVE   E

FRANKLIN STOVE   LITTLE JOE

"Boatman's Choice"

A, B, and D were the stoves used on the decks of barges. C, E, F, and G were generally used in the cabins. The seven types shown here were not the only stoves used, but are representative of the numerous styles that were available.

Barge life was simple because it had to be. The boats moved continuously from four a.m. until 10 p.m. when the locks closed. (Before 1855 they moved all through the night.) Only on Sundays did they come to rest and this was the day for general cleanup. Barges were scrubbed, minor repairs made. The women did the weekly wash and if the weather was nice, hung it to dry on lines strung up on the deck. If the weather was foul, they moved the washing operation into the cabin and hung the clothes in the steerage.

The day started with a hearty breakfast — probably ham and eggs, home fried potatoes, thick slices of homemade bread. Plenty of coffee was always available. Milk and other perishables were bought frequently at the farms along the route, since the barges had no refrigeration.

The midday dinner and evening meals were usually substantial as well. On a hot day a cold meal might be served so the cabin would not get heated up by the stove. Beef, pork, ham, and fish were frequently on the menu along with the vegetables that kept best — cabbage, beans, potatoes, turnips, corn, and beets. Salt pork and salt mackerel were favorites since they didn't spoil easily. Salted meat was sometimes hung in the space between the two sections of squeezer barges, but if it was not watched carefully, eels would nibble it down to nothing. Now and then the boatmen found the food monotonous. On one occasion the crew on a carpenter boat asked their cook to try something different for dessert. The cook, not being a very bright fellow, asked what they wanted. Stace Dillon, well known for his kidding around, said, "How about rice pudding with onions?" That's what the cook served, and both cook and pudding ended up in the Canal.

At least this particular crew (traveling without family) had a cook. On other boats with all-male crews the stove was frequently put near the steersman. He had to cook, steer the barge and serve the meals. Then, as was customary on boats where only the minimum crew of two was on board, he would switch places with the mule tender walking on the towpath. All this was done without stopping the boat. Sometimes the steersman pole-vaulted over the water to the mule tender's spot and the mule tender vaulted back to the rudder, but usually it was a two- or three-foot jump. After dark, they were aided by a night-hawker, a type of lantern which was an important part of every boat's equipment.

One of the old timers' stories was about the Miller brothers, Levi, "Whiskey Jack," and Benny. One bright, moonlight night, Benny, using his night-hawker, was passing under a bridge. A group of boys on the bridge threw stones at the barge and yelled, "What's the matter, Benny, can't you see in the moonlight?" Fortunately for these rowdies, Benny couldn't get to them from his boat, for the Millers were known as a tough bunch of men, and the kids would probably have found themselves in the Canal.

Another bargeman, Reuben Nace, carried a shotgun loaded with rock salt, and didn't hesitate to use it on anyone who stood on the bridges kicking dirt and stones on the men eating their meal on deck. Things like this usually happened in the coal area of the Canal operation.

The story is told that one farmer who lived alongside the Canal used to tie a monkey to a post near the bank. Passing bargemen would amuse themselves throwing coal at the monkey, providing a little extra fuel for the farmer.

The men who owned mules and ran barges took great pride in the strength, durability, and operating efficiency of both, but they weren't known as fancy dressers. Oscar Geddes was an exception, according to an old Scotsman who told me about him: "Aye, he was the best dom' dressed mon that walked a pair of mules, and ye couldn't sell his mules short — they looked almost as good as he did. He was a big mon, too — always fixed up to please the ladies — had a beard that was the envy of everyone. No matter how muddy or dusty the towpath was, his boots were always polished. Every year he would refinish and repaint his boat. She was a picture going down the Canal with shiny brass bells on the harness of his mules, tinkling as they walked. Yessiree! It was a fine sight to see Oscar and his mules coming down the towpath."

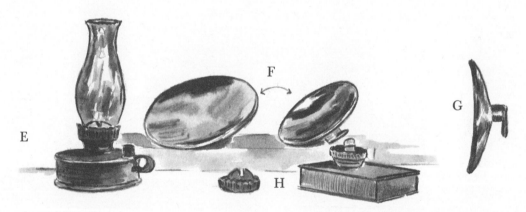

A and B show lamps with attached reflectors. C and D are the same lamps without reflectors. E, F, G, and H further illustrate parts of a night-hawker. G shows side view of a reflector. The tongue fitted into a groove on the inside of the back of the lantern. I shows the night-hawker completely assembled and J is the same one without its interior parts. K shows the extended metal pieces on the bottom of the night-hawker which kept the kerosene lamp from upsetting as the barge moved or was bumped.

The "Night-hawker" and its component parts.

    Here are various types of night-hawkers. There were others, of course, but the basic structure and design followed the pattern of those illustrated. Probably one of the earliest was that used by Levi Winters (L,M) showing back and front of the same lantern. Whale oil and camphor were first used for fuel. The tubes along the side carried heat given off by the lamp within to a one-inch enclosed space in the bottom of the lantern. This kept the whale oil or camphor from hardening on cold nights. Later kerosene was used and this of course did not harden.

The Scotsman continued, "Then there was that fellow Henry Noggles, he was a real powerful mon, too, must have been six foot two or three. Ugliest mon I ever saw, big feet and a big nose, and hands like a gorilla. You know, I don't believe I ever saw him mad, or in trouble — seems like every time Henry came around, people just stayed out of his way and gave him plenty of room. Why, he was gentle as a kitten with his mules — I never saw him use a whip or be rough with them like some fellows did. No matter how busy he was, he would always give a fellow a hand on a big load, but he sure was no John Gilbert."

The women of the Canal families were as rugged and hard-working as their men. Jim Magill, who spent much of his boyhood on the banks of the Canal, recalls an incident that made a lasting impression on him. Jim's father was a stocky, redheaded, outspoken country doctor, well liked by the canallers. Once, as Jim watched a barge pull into the New Hope coal yard, the barge captain yelled to him, "Fetch your dad quick, son. My wife's below expecting a baby!"

Doc Magill came on the double, making it just in time to deliver the baby, then went off on his rounds. Next morning, after the coal had been unloaded, the barge started its trip back to Easton, the new father driving the mules and the mother at the tiller steering the boat.

Old bargemen love to get together and reminisce, and it is a rare treat to be with them at such a time. Once when Frank Sigafoos and John O. McEntee were talking I heard about John Reigal. John always carried a pouch of gold pieces around with him, and settled his debts in gold. Friends warned him that this was not a safe practice, so John, who distrusted banks, finally made some inquiries among those he considered the more reliable citizens and businessmen in the Uhlerstown area; would it be safe to put the money in a bank and would he surely be able to get it back when he wanted it? They assured him it would be much safer than carrying it around, and would even grow. They urged him not to delay, as there were highway bandits operating in the countryside. The

63

next day the anxious Reigal deposited $1,600, all in gold pieces — a tidy sum to have saved, working on the Canal.

Next Mr. Mc Entee had the floor. "Remember Old Charlie Tiger? 'Captain Charlie' they called him sometimes, and sometimes just plain 'Tiger.' He had a heavy beard all over his face — thick hair that went in all directions and big bushy eyebrows. Made you think of the Black Pirate when he glowered at you. Well sir, one day Captain Charlie let his boat get out of control on the Lehigh and a heavy wind blew him and his boat over the dam, and it wedged in a rock formation. They say you could hear Charlie for a mile away yelling, 'Halp! Halp! Come save me, halp save a Deutschlander.'"

Mr. McEntee chuckled, relit his pipe, pondered a moment, looked over at Frank and said, "And how about that fellow named King Crow, I never did know his right name. They nicknamed him that because he was always telling such tall stories. One day he went in a grocery store and asked for a dozen black hen eggs. The keeper of the store scratched his head and said he couldn't tell the difference. 'Well set 'em on the counter,' said the King 'and I'll show you.' Willing to learn, the keeper of the store set the big basket of eggs on the counter while King Crow proceeded to pick out a dozen of the largest eggs, placing them in a bag and paying the regular price, he said, 'The black hens always lay the biggest eggs!'"

Frank Sigafoos had still another yarn. One day, he said, while he was taking a work horse to a pasture, the dredge, with a full crew of men and Stace Dillon in charge, was moving up the Canal. The dredge carries a derrick with a clam and it can only be moved a short distance at a time. It is operated by steam power, and the boiler is built with a kicker to it. As the kicker goes into action it shoves the dredge forward a few feet, then the boiler has to build up enough steam to send the kicker into action again. This is a slow and tedious method of moving the dredge up to a new working area, which is usually only a few yards ahead.

Stace yelled to Frank for a little help to speed things up. Frank threw a rope to the dredge and fastened his end to the traces of the horse, and was about to do his good deed when a fancy carriage came along carrying four dressed-up women. The carriage stopped, and with all four of the women glaring at Frank, one of them said, "Don't you dare make that little horse pull that big dredge! Unhitch it at once or I'll call the police." The horse was unhitched and the dredge continued kicking its way up the Canal. The four large women in the heavy carriage went their way. "And," said Frank, "that horse they had hitched to that carriage wasn't much bigger than a good-sized pony."

Frank Sigafoos

Stace Dillon used to come down to my studio and model for the art students. He had the rugged leatherlike skin of the river man and at some time in his life he had lost an eye, which had been replaced with a glass eye. When Stace was modeling, he would take out the eye, cock his hat on the side of his head and relax, enjoying himself while the class studied him.

Stace died a few years ago, but his wife Liz, also a colorful character, still lives in their house opposite Lock No. 10, one of the wide water areas in the lock system through New Hope. Liz can tell you off with words that make your hair curl.

I stop in once in a while to say hello to Liz, and one day mentioned the barges that used to run the Canal. "Don't tell me about them things," said Liz. "Why, I nearly drowned jumping off one of them damn boats." There were usually several barges tied up near the Dillons' place, and a good deal of bantering went on. This day Liz was standing on a barge, and one of the bargemen dared her to jump into the Canal. The boat wasn't loaded, which set it up fairly high in the water. But nobody in his right mind dares Liz.

"I guess this fellow wasn't in his right mind that day," Liz went on. "Anyway, I jumped and went head first into the silt of the Canal bed, which hadn't been dredged lately. When I finally came up, the men were getting ready to dive in and look for me. I sure thought I was a goner that day!"

Stace once told me his folks were the famous Dillons of the West, and when he would tell his yarns of the past, he would remove his glass eye and squint at you, looking for all the world like Long John Silver. No one ever questioned Long John, and I wasn't about to question Stace.

During the nonoperating months, the Canal families lived on their own farms or in boardinghouses. Men who traveled without their families during the season could see them from time to time on a Sunday if their boats were tied up close enough to home.

Children traveling on the Canal with their parents had no formal school-

66

Liz Dillon

ing during the season. But, living as close to nature as they did, they learned things other youngsters were denied. Fishing and swimming were at their doorstep and former barge children, themselves now grandparents, nostalgically recall falling off to sleep listening to the lapping water and the nocturnal songs of frogs, crickets, katydids, and whippoorwills, and watching the stars moving across the sky, seeming close enough to touch. Naturally, many of these children developed a great love for life on the Canal and continued in their parents' occupation. Sometimes, though, the children had other ideas, and went into other fields. It could be the other way around too. Harry Warford, now close to ninety, who worked on the Canal for fifty years, tells a story about one of the two men whose job it was in later years to ferry the barges from one outlet to the other in the New Hope-Lambertville interchange. Joe Denson's father was a shoe-maker in New Hope and as a teenager Joe was being groomed to follow in his footsteps. Joe much preferred the idea of working on the Canal.

On one occasion, Joe's father told the boy to take a burlap bag, go to the boat yard, and bring it back full of shavings. Joe took the bag and left, but in-stead of filling it, hid the empty bag in a remote section of the boat yard. Then he ran off and apparently was not missed to any extent. He reappeared two years later, and remembering the bag of shavings he had been sent to fetch, he found the bag where he had hidden it, filled it with shavings, and headed back to his father's shop. He dropped the bag on the floor. His father, who was working, looked up; all he said was, "It took you a hell of a while to get them."

Life on and around the Canal was usually pleasantly predictable. Lucy White's recollections give one a feeling of what it must have been like.

Lucy was eight years old when her mother died. Her father decided to devote the rest of his life to boating on the Canal. He took his five children and established residence at Point Pleasant. "Hackey" Samsel hired Lucy's father to operate one of his fleet of canal boats. Clara, the oldest child, took care of the baby and domestic chores while the three other children took turns accom-panying their father on barge trips and helping out by acting as helmsmen or walking the mules. Though they usually carried coal, sometimes they had a dif-ferent cargo. They might start out early in the morning and head for the quarry above Lambertville, New Jersey. There the boat would be loaded with trap rock for shipment to Philadelphia. Or sometimes they used the feeder canal on the Jersey side and headed for Trenton and the Raritan Canal which eventually opened into the Raritan Basin at New Brunswick.

It was a two-day haul to New Brunswick if time were pressing and no stops made. Otherwise, they would stop at Trenton where the Canal was bordered with facilities for boats to hook up and lodging and meals. Upon arrival at the

Lucy White

Raritan Basin, their boat would join the others waiting for a tug to pull the lot of them down to Philadelphia. Lucy's father would stay with the boat, sending Lucy and her older brother to ride the team of mules back to Trenton, over the bridge and on to Bristol. There they waited for her father and the empty barge, one of several being towed back to the Bristol Basin.

The barge was quickly hooked to the team, went through Lock No. 1 and then on to Easton via the Delaware Division Canal. Their destination might be a coal loading station below Mauch Chunk on the Lehigh River. Here, a chute would be placed from the trap doors of the coal carriers into the barge hold. About half an hour was required to place and fill each section. Two coal cars filled both sections of a barge.

Raubsville fall gate. The upper part is the gate section, the lower a solid, fixed section whose height is that of the drop from one level to the next. Wicket openings can be seen at bottom. On the wall are cleats for tying barges within the lock.

Interior of lock tender's building. The small cranberry glass window with shelf to support kerosene lamp was used to warn bargemen traveling at night that locks were closed. When lamp was removed, barges were free to come through.

It was very important to load quickly, and get out and on the way before another bargeman waiting to be loaded would finish, catch up, enter the double lock, then pass you in the next level. If you arrived at a set of locks five minutes before 10 p.m. you could go through. A boat five or ten minutes in back of you would have to wait until 4 a.m., as all locks closed promptly. This gave the boat just passing through a few hours lead, depending on the length of the level he was in.

The trip to Bristol was usually uneventful, although occasionally there was trouble of one sort or another. For one thing, mules tended to wander to the side; bushes and flowers tempted them. Hitched together as they were for long hours, the routine doubtless became monotonous, even to a mule. The types of diversion in which a bored mule might indulge were somewhat limited and the usual one was to bite the nearest thing — the rump of the mule directly ahead. The offended animal would then let fly with both hoofs and kick his teammate. If it were a three-mule hookup, the third animal would be so startled out of his complacent plodding, he might begin to buck and bray. All three usually ended up in the Canal. Everything became bedlam — water splashing in all directions, mules braying and kicking, men shouting, the barge half turned looking as if it were considering joining the fun. Eventually order was restored, the harness was salvaged and repaired, and the barge continued on its way.

A coal shipment might be delivered to Yardley, Morrisville, Bristol, or taken by tug to Philadelphia. Bargemen at one time received $1.00 per ton for delivering coal, consequently they loaded their barges to capacity, trying to get as near one hundred tons as possible. Later on, as the Canal bed filled in and allowed less draft for boats, loads had to be cut by several tons.

Northampton Cement Mills shipped considerable cement by barge. Chutes carried the hot bags of cement to the hold. Teams of men with heavy leather-palmed gloves would catch these bags as they slid down, stacking them as fast as they could. It was a nasty and dangerous job. When a barge was loaded, the heat from the fresh cement made it impossible to stay below decks, even in the cabin.

On one occasion, young Willie White and his father were delivering a fresh load of this hot stuff to St. Georges, Delaware, for construction of a lock in the

A cantankerous mule upsets the serenity of a bargeman's life.

Chesapeake Canal. A heavy storm was roughing up the water, visibility was poor, and the tug pulling them had extended its tow line to keep as far as possible from the loaded barge. Waves were slapping the deck with great force and sometimes engulfed the entire boat. The youngster was plain scared as the barge lurched, dipped, and swayed in the rough water.

The tug captain, too, was having problems of his own. Buoy markers could not be seen and the extended tow line caught in the propeller of the tug, causing him to lose control of the towed barge which promptly got caught on a sand bar. After a hazardous time, the barge was pulled free and with a shortened tow line both boats finally made a safe harbor where they tied up until the storm abated.

January 8, 1841, was the night of a memorable storm. On January 9, 1841, David Connor of the Superintendent's office at Easton wrote to the Canal Commissioners:

> I hasten to give you a short sketch of the condition in which a large number of the sections of the Delaware Division Pennsylvania Canal is at the present, occasioned by the flood on the 8th inst. The water in the Delaware and Lehigh rivers rose so rapidly on the eve of the 7th inst., and speedily inundated the lower part of our town, so that it was with difficulty that those living in that section escaped with their lives, their property nearly all destroyed. The Delaware rose to the unprecedented height of 32 feet, which is seven feet higher than it was ever known to have been within the recollection of the oldest inhabitants. The bridge across the Lehigh at this place has been swept away, and in fact every other bridge on the Lehigh so far as we can learn. . . .
>
> The damage sustained by the Delaware Canal . . . will exceed that of the spring of 1839 so far as could be ascertained as yet.
>
> The new dam has been but slightly injured, but the whole of the embankment around the basin together with the Collector's Office and Lock House have been swept away, leaving the outlet lock standing bare, the whole current of the Lehigh running through between the dam and the Outlet Lock into the Delaware. I cannot as yet give you a detailed account of the extent of the damages sustained as the water is not low enough to make a thorough examination but will endeavor to do so soon.

Another superintendent, Daniel Y. Harman, wrote of the same flood:

> I hasten to inform you that we have one of the most awful rivers that has

73

been known by our oldest residents. . . . It has swept all before it. All the bridges from Easton to Trenton are swept clear. Houses and barns and even men were swept down the furious element.

One man who was on the Center Bridge [a covered bridge] at the time it moved off went with the same and was carried with the current 17 miles before he could be taken off, which fortunately was effected. . . . The mail is waiting, excuse haste.

Another bad storm occurred in 1862. Many boats were washed aground and passengers drowned either through the force of the storm or because they couldn't swim. After the storm dead animal cargoes were found floating in the river. Wrecked boats were left to rot. It took five years for the area to recover from the calamity.

Nature in a less outraged mood produced a number of occupations on the Canal. The Canal Company had to keep a dredger working throughout the season to clear the silt which accumulated from the streams emptying into the Canal. Four men usually worked the dredger. Like the boatmen, they lived on the Canal in season, although their quarters were in a separate craft attached to the dredger. They, too, took off for their own homes when they were near enough and they managed to get in more such visits than the bargeman since they worked a shorter day—from 8 A.M. to 6 P.M. Each dredge was equipped with a derrick and a clam used to clean the sides and bottom of the Canal. The dredge itself was about 10 feet in width. A flat-bottomed scow, about five feet wide, was hooked to each side, balancing the dredge and preventing it from tipping as a clam brought up a load and deposited it in a hollow scow which carried it to the dumping ground and then returned for the next load. This maintenance crew had right of way over all traffic on the Canal. Dredging was apparently hungry work; Flora Henry remembers one occasion when a dredger was at Smithdown for two weeks and the men aboard paid her to bring them

fresh bread. The crew of four consumed fifteen loaves of bread a week plus buns. Miss Henry also recalls that it took three lockages to get the complicated dredger through to the next section of the Canal. It was possible, however, for the two balanced barges to be hooked, side by side, onto the back of the dredger and put all three sections through at once, using three or four mules.

Harvey Eichlin

Harvey Eichlin, now in his eighties, spent thirty-six years with the Lehigh Coal and Navigation Company. At one point he worked on a dredger. He and Stace Dillon were classified as engineers and worked a double shift, sharing the foremanship. One took charge while the other ate and slept, twelve hours each shift when the pressure was on. Harvey not only worked as an engineer, but also served as trainman, the crewman who controlled the bucket on the dredger, or as the fireman, who kept the boiler going. Or he worked as the mule skinner, whose job it was to move from place to place, plus other incidental jobs. In fact Harvey worked wherever he was needed most.

Mr. Eichlin recalls the time, around 1904, when the Lehigh Company experimented with tugboats as a substitute for mules. A tug would pull a line of five or six barges. "But," as Mr. Eichlin put it, "a quart of oats and ten cents' worth of hay for a mule was about the cheapest transportation you could get."

During the period when tugboats were in use, Mr. Eichlin was captain of a crew that pulled barges between Easton and Bristol. He had a man at the tiller of each barge to keep them in line. It was a long and lonesome trip, and

A tugboat pulls a line of barges. Tugs were used for only two years after which the mules again took over.

the men would sometimes ease the boredom by taking frequent nips from the ever-present bottle. Barges would begin to waver and ram into the bank, and Mr. Eichlin would have to pull them all over to the side and straighten everybody out.

On arriving at Bristol, the crew would take off for the local taverns and a well-earned break. When the time came for the return trip, Mr. Eichlin would hire a wagon, make the rounds of the taverns, and collect his crew. Sometimes it took a fight to get a bargeman back on the job.

Barge captains who brought coal and other commodities down from Easton always tried to get a cargo which would make the return trip profitable.

A carpenter boat leaving Lock No. 13.

If this happened to be watermelons, an all-night guard would have to be posted whenever the barge tied up, but it is said that a good many guards happened to be looking the other way when boys would sneak up in the dark to get themselves a melon or two.

Carpenter boats were flat-ended scows and were fitted out to look like houseboats. Materials for general repairs tools, workbenches and replacement parts were on board. The housekeeping arrangements were similar to those on the barge, but the "boatman's choice" was larger, having four lids and an oven.

Carpenter boats worked up and down the Canal, repairing bridges, the towpath, locks, company houses and barns along the way, cutting down trees and performing numerous other jobs. Sometimes as many as fourteen or fifteen men made up a crew, staying with the boat from Monday through Saturday, working hard, eating heartily, and sleeping soundly.

When a serious leak was found in the Canal bed, the crew built a temporary dam around the trouble spot, leaving enough room for a barge to pass. This area was then pumped out, rocks laid in to form a base for well-soaked straw or leaves to be packed into all the crevices, followed by a good coating of clay, well tamped, as the final layer. When hard, the dam wall was removed. Small holes were simply packed with straw and clay.

In Harrisburg they still laugh over a story told about Russ Paetzel's ingenuity in fixing a leak. At the Stony Brook aqueduct below Brownsburg there had been trouble with a large hole in the base. Everything the repair crew tried washed through. Russ, who was superintendent, spotted a discarded bedspring near the canal one day while he was looking things over. He threw the spring into the opening as a base for corn fodder and clay and it did the trick. The patch-up job lasted for many years and Russ is still turning down offers of old bedsprings.

Many of the leaks were caused by muskrats. They burrowed holes in the banks and bottom, allowing the precious water to escape. Muskrats were so

Repair work on the overflow control gate at New Hope. The tractor-drawn derrick and clam are on the towpath level. Russ Paetzel, who was superintendent of the Canal between Easton and Bristol, discusses with the operator how closely they can dig to the stone wall without undermining it. A cement mixer next to the derrick pours its load down the trough into a waiting wheelbarrow, while the workmen reset and cross-hatch the creosoted ties and patch the wall section along the sides. Across the Canal to the left is the house occupied by Harry Warford.

SAND
BAGS

Joe Agosta, foreman of the maintenance crew, directing repair work on the fall gate at Raubsville. The gate chain gave way while they were cleaning out and Joe and his helper were almost caught under the eight-ton gate as it dropped. There was just enough water in the pocket of the wickets to slow the falling gate and push the men out of danger. Sand bags stacked along the Canal bed limit water flow in the work areas.

bothersome that the Lehigh Coal and Navigation Co. offered $1.50 each for their pelts. A constant battle was also fought with snakes, crayfish, eels, and moles, which jammed mechanisms and were generally ever-present trouble makers.

Barge approaching Lock No. 8. The small boat tied to a snubbing post is a "flicker."

Another maintenance boat was the "flicker." Its one-man crew had the job of keeping the Canal banks clean, cutting grass, weeds, bushes, and tree branches that hampered the movement of the mules and barges, filling in holes on the towpath, and reporting places where repairs beyond their limitations were needed. These boats were about four feet wide and eighteen to twenty feet long. They had oars and a pole for moving around from one bank to another, but a mule or horse was used to pull it from one work location to another. In fact, mules or horses, usually mules, were always used in moving all types of boats — barges, derricks, scows, and carpenter boats — when they had to go any distance.

The lockkeeper had one of the most important jobs on the Canal. Flora Henry's father, Jake Henry, was for many years the lockkeeper at the double lock at Smithtown, and his daughter learned most of the tricks of the trade. Since the barges had no regular schedule, the lockkeeper had to judge by the sound of the conch horn the direction from which the barge was coming and how far away it was. Then he would reply with a blast on a bugle or whistle — one blast for all clear and three for hold up. If all was well, an efficient lockkeeper could have his lock filled and ready by the time the barge was ready to enter it. It was not only the lockkeeper's duty to operate the lock gates, but to keep the overflow control gate properly set, see that the sluiceways were clean and in good working order, and report damages or leaks.

During a downpour Jake Henry would usually go a few hundred yards up the towpath and work the waste gate, which allowed an overflow to empty into a creek and ultimately the river. For this job he was paid the standard section gang wage, four dollars a day, and was provided with a small building for drying off. If a barge arrived while Jake Henry was thus occupied, the barge would have to hold up until Jake returned from the waste gate. A barn near the towpath provided shelter for the mules and the bargemen could retire to the warmth of their cabins.

During the winter, lock tenders helped in the repair of the Canal. The Canal was emptied at that time to prevent it from freezing over and to allow the men to free the banks of muskrat holes which caused an estimated $5,000 worth of damage every year. During the off season Jake Henry sometimes worked on the highways — which eventually helped make the Canals obsolete. He also cut ice in the river and filled icehouses along the way.

Like all lockkeepers, the Henrys lived rent free in a house owned by the

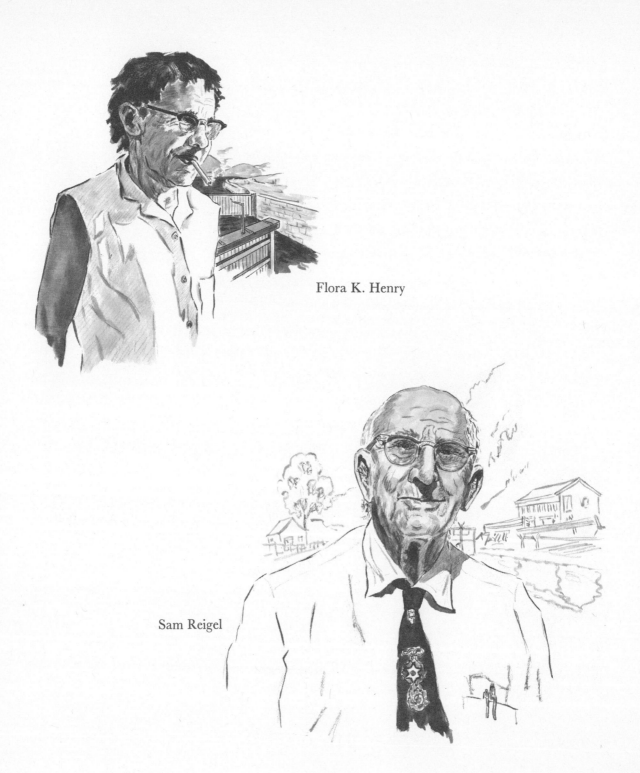

Flora K. Henry

Sam Reigel

84

Canal Commission. The houses were mostly of saltbox design, made of fieldstone or else of frame construction, with the necessary outbuildings.

A number of other occupations were associated with the Canal. Sam Reigel at the age of 93 recollected his years of work at the Uhlerstown boat yard. He began in 1909 and by the time he left in 1921 he had been foreman for some time and was earning 58¢ an hour. The workmen were paid 40¢ an hour. From five to seven men worked in the yard and took about two hundred days to complete a boat. During Mr. Reigel's tenure an average of one boat a year was constructed. It could be expected to last from twenty-five to thirty years. Much of the work in the yard consisted of maintenance and repair on boats already built. Crews also built bridges and aqueducts as they were needed. Between Easton and Bristol, for instance, there were nine aqueducts and 106 bridges. Horace Sigafoos, who is now known for the handsome scale models he has made of bridges and boats, has pointed out that the balance of stresses make the camelback bridges an outstanding engineering achievement. Horace is now a patrol officer of the Theodore Roosevelt State Park.

Harry Warford was at one time in charge of the entire Canal section around New Hope, and he has held almost every position that existed on the Canal. He was also mayor of New Hope, and one of the most popular officials the town ever had. Mr. Warford is considered one of the best living authorities on the operation of the Delaware Division. One day he demonstrated to me his ability to blow the conch horn, and the blast almost knocked my ears off. "If you think one of these sea shell horns is easy to blow," he said, "just try it!"

Harry Warford started his long career on the Canal in 1907. He remembers that in those days the Canal employed five carpenters, a blacksmith, eight bank bosses, and three watchmen. Each bank boss was responsible for a section of the Canal and supervised three workers who cut the grass. The watchmen's prime duties were performed during heavy showers when the stream came up so high it was necessary to put up the wastegate.

Half section of a "squeezer" barge under construction at the Uhlerstown Boat Yard.

Front section of the same barge nearly completed.

Barge passing under camelback bridge and through wicket gate of Lock No. 8.

Mr. Warford also remembers the great volume of business generated by the traffic on the Canal. Among the shops in the New Hope area listed in an old almanac are the Defiance Cigar Store, the Logan House, George Reinert, baker and confectioner, and T. E. Watson's for "the best smoking and chewing tobacco." Also in town were a cotton manufacturer, a harness maker, a foundry, a flax factory, a fishery, livery stables, a jeweler, a shoemaker, a milliner, a lumber merchant, and four doctors.

A lively business was done in mule trading. A good team of mules would cost between $300 and $400, and their quality was a source of great pride to the bargeman. Many a fist fight started with an argument over whose team was the best. Changes to fresh mules were made at times, but generally each opera-

Harry Warford blows the "conch," which signalled the bargeman's approach to a lock.

Various kinds of horns used. One bargeman was known for using a bugle.

88

tor owned his team and they did the job on the entire trip. Barns at key points along the Canal supplied grain and fodder for the mules, and rented stalls for housing them in bad weather. Twenty-five cents would buy a day's feed for two mules.

According to one old timer, mules brought better prices at auctions than horses because of their strength, stamina, and better natures. If a mischievous boy threw a stone at a barge and it hit a mule instead, the mule would just flick its ears and move a little faster, whereas a horse would jump and cause trouble.

Naturally, all the activity on and around the Canal required official regulations, and this was the province of the Canal Commission. Bargemen were subject to a special set of laws and were fined for violations, the amounts depending on the seriousness of the offense. Bickering or brawling were causes for fines and one of the heaviest fines would be levied against an operator who failed to yield the right of way. Flora Henry recalls one pair of boatmen who

Artist's conception of a mule auction at Uhlerstown. Mules were brought in by the dealer and kept in enclosures for prospective buyers to look over and decide on their choices when bidding got under way.

took advantage of her sex and flaunted the rules of lockage. She reported the miscreants to the Canal boss, who caught up with them and administered both a good bawling out and a stiff fine. Each year the Canal supervisors made nominations for lockkeepers, submitting their recommendations to the Canal Commission, which had to approve them.

Letters kept on file in the Journal of the Canal Commission in Harrisburg are written proof that from its very inception the Canal Commission was harassed with injunctions, damage claims, lawsuits about property rights and many other matters. For example, the following letter dated in 1834 while the Canal was being built appears in a Canal Commission journal:

> The President laid before the Board the claim of Joseph Warner of $815.00 compensation, for injury to corn meal by an obstacle in passage of waste weir of his mill, occasioned by the Delaware Division and for raising dam. Which was read and considered and on motion resolved unanimously that claim of Joseph Warner ought not to be allowed. The damage to his mill and water power have been settled upon an appeal to the appraisers.

On March 26, 1844, Martin Coreyell wrote to the Honorable Joseph Miller of the Canal Commission, objecting to Joseph Hough's holding a job as foreman on the Canal, due to his heavy drinking, reminding them that he was given the job out of charity for his family, and that he had not reformed.

On March 25, 1844, William Horn, collector at the Bristol Basin, wrote the Canal Commission referring to the fact that fifteen million feet of lumber passed through the Canal in the previous year. He made comparisons of costs on lumber and coal: A boat carrying forty thousand feet of lumber worth $12 per thousand comes to $480, and at 4 mills pays $9.60 toll, while 60 tons of coal pays $16.30 toll, and at $3.00 a ton is worth $180. A statement made out on bills collected from the Lehigh Coal and Navigation Company in the year 1843 reads as follows:

No. of Boats	Mauch Chunk Weight	Easton Weight	Toll Collected
1503	86,220-2/3 tons	89,730-14/20 tons	$25,916.59

A letter in the Pennsylvania Archives tells us of one noncommercial activity of the Canal. On November 11, 1844, Capt. Samuel Dickinson wrote the Canal Commissioners at Harrisburg requesting permission to transport forty National Guardsmen from Trenton to Easton through the Delaware Division, "to inspire military ardor and increase the spirit in promoting volunteers. Therefore pray that in consideration of our laudable purpose, you will permit us to pass toll free on said canal on this date." The captain's request was granted.

A barge party in the early nineteen-hundreds, getting ready for a day's outing. This actually is a scow, which was generally used for such occasions. The scow was washed out and poles were set in the sides and a canopy drawn over for shade. A bargeman who owned a team of mules was hired by the hour for the excursion.

Approaching Raubsville on the way to Bristol. At the left is the Raubsville Power Plant, at the right a lockkeeper's shanty. A stone-faced wall divided the Canal as it reached this point, part of it flowing to the Power Plant, the rest continuing through the locks. Water flow and pressure were stronger between Easton and Raubsville than in any other section of the Canal.

Intake and control wheels of the Raubsville Power Plant.

Sluiceway from Power Plant returning excess and waste water to the Canal.

Delaware River outlet of Raubsville Power Plant. Water passing through turbines produced current for operating trolley service from Easton to Doylestown and was returned through this outlet to the river.

Life on the Canal had its difficulties, and the work was hard, but it was also a sociable existence. On weekends and holidays, relatives and friends visited, and boatmen tied up together during a delay visited back and forth. Since the men didn't have much spending money, one of the favorite diversions along with conversation was playing pinochle. Sometimes, if a boat had to lay over for a time, for excitement, a captain of one boat would issue a challenge to a captain of another to see who had the best fighter in his crew. Each fighter was warned the loser would get no supper that night. These were bare knuckles affairs with rather vague rules. But no loser was ever known to faint from hunger.

Taverns along the route became favorite gathering places. The River House at New Hope near Lock No. 8 was one of these. Although officially a general store, men and mules could bed down for the night and drinking, gabbing and fighting were accepted pastimes. A woman known as Madge ran this emporium of gaiety. She weighed about three hundred pounds and could hold her own with any man in a knock-down, drag-out brawl. On one occasion, apparently Madge had been hitting the bottle with more than her customary enthusiasm and came bouncing out from behind the counter. While the men clapped and whistled she did the Irish jig. The flooring of the River House creaked and sagged as first toes then heels tapped away.

Another Canal legend concerns Jesse Mason, a strapping six-footer. One would think twice before crossing him. It seems one fellow bargeman wasn't too good at thinking and when Jesse came home from a barge trip he found this chap with his wife. Going to the barn, he grabbed an ax, followed the fellow and split his head open. Before Jess could sell his belongings and leave town, friends of the victim, not seeing him around for a couple of days, started looking and found the body. The rest was pieced together quickly enough for the sheriff to arrest Jesse.

The trial was held at Doylestown, and the verdict was "Hang until dead."

Jesse didn't seem too disturbed; he joked with the keepers, ate well, and advertised in the local papers for his remains to be sold and used for medical research.

A Dr. Johnson paid the fifty dollars for these rights. There was snow the day of the hanging and the doctor loaded Jesse's body in the back of his sleigh and took off for home. It was mighty cold on the country road so the doctor stopped on the way for a shot of whiskey. The innkeeper poured his drink and looking out the window, said, "Say, ain't that fellow cold laying out there in the sleigh?" "Yup," the doctor replied. "Guess he is." The innkeeper, being a sympathetic soul, poured a drink and proceeded to take it out to the poor man. Dashing in with a scared wide-eyed look on his face, he yelled "That guy's dead." "Yup," said Doc, and finishing his drink walked to the sleigh, hopped in and headed for home.

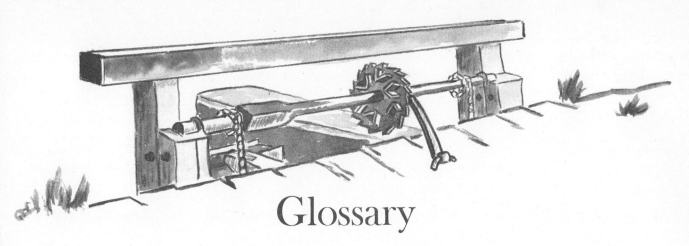

Glossary

Aqueduct: a structure made of steel, stone or wood, for conveying a canal over a river, creek, or hollow.

Basin: a large water enclosure to one side of a canal where barges can be repaired, docked, or tied up, before continuing their trip—a kind of water parking lot.

Berm bank: the bank opposite the towpath.

Bump bridge: a bridge that works on the principle of swinging doors. Nudged or "bumped" in the center by a barge, the hinged sides swing open for passage, and close again when the barge is clear, allowing normal bridge traffic to resume.

Camel-back bridge: a rigid bridge, high enough for barge clearance.

Canal: an artificial waterway for navigation, for drainage, or for irrigating land.

Canal boat: almost any boat used within the canal area for transportation of cargo; a name often used for a large barge.

Canaller: one whose livelihood depends on the canal. Sometimes called canawler.

Chunker: nickname for barges with cargoes of coal from Mauch Chunk, Pennsylvania.

Dog house: the housing for the mechanism of the wicket gate.

Driver: one who drives the mules or horses pulling the barges. Also called a skinner.

Drop gate: see fall gate.

Fall gate, or drop gate: a single unit gate weighing several tons and always located at the upper end of a lock area. It is raised and lowered by water pressure and heavy chains attached to wheels that start momentum. (See illustrations for full details.)

Feeder: a branch transportation line; also a narrow channel of water bypassing a lock and flowing into the next level.

Flicker: on the Delaware Canal, a small flat-bottomed boat, square at both ends and used in loading or unloading. On the Morris Canal, and some others, a small-capacity, single-unit scow. Also called a lighter.

Hinge boat: a barge constructed in two separate sections, each with its own cargo space. The bow is pointed, the stern section square. Movable bars that slide into couplings hold the two sections together. This can also be done by hawsers wrapped around cleats.

Inclined plane: a sloping track surface fitted with cradles which hold barges and haul them by cable over steep or rough terrain to join another section of the regular canal where locks would have been impractical. Used on the Morris Canal and the Pennsylvania Canal.

Level: same as open water.

Lock: an enclosure in a canal, with a gate at each end. Used for raising or lowering boats passing from level to level.

Lock house, or lockkeeper's house: lockkeeper's rent-free home.

Lockkeeper, or lock tender: one who operates a lock.

Lock shanty: at fall gate of lock. Houses gears for the gate, and is a temporary shelter for lockkeeper in bad weather.

Locking through: the process of moving from level to level using water pressure within the locks.

Open water: the canal between lock areas. Also called a level.

Prism: cross-section diagram of a canal.

Puddling: wet mixture of clay, sand, and limestone applied to the canal bed and allowed to dry hard in the sun.

Ratter: a muskrat trapper, paid a bounty of about 18 cents per tail. He averaged 10-15 destructive rodents per day—good pay.

Rip rap: a stone facing on the banks for strength and to reduce erosion.

Skinner: see driver.

Scow gang: maintenance men.

Sluice gate: gate for regulating waterflow through a sluiceway bypassing the lock. Also called waste gate, and waste weir.

Snubbing post: a post around which a rope is thrown to check a boat's momentum.

Squeezer: a hinge boat.

Stiff: a single-unit barge.

Tiller: a lever for turning the rudder of a barge.

Toll house: where boats are weighed, fees collected, and records kept.

Towline or towrope: a rope tied from mules to barges for towing.

Towpath: bank of the canal where mules and drivers walk, opposite the berm bank.

Wicket: a small rectangular opening within the lock area, usually at the bottom of a wicket gate. It controls the flow of water when the gate is closed. A long rod extends from the top of the wicket gate to a coupling on the opening. By turning the rod a small amount of water is let through a lock; the water level reaches a greater depth in the lock area when the wicket is closed.

Winch: an instrument, such as a crank, for hauling or pulling.

Wing dam: a pier built from the shore to deepen a channel or to divert logs or boats.

Appendix

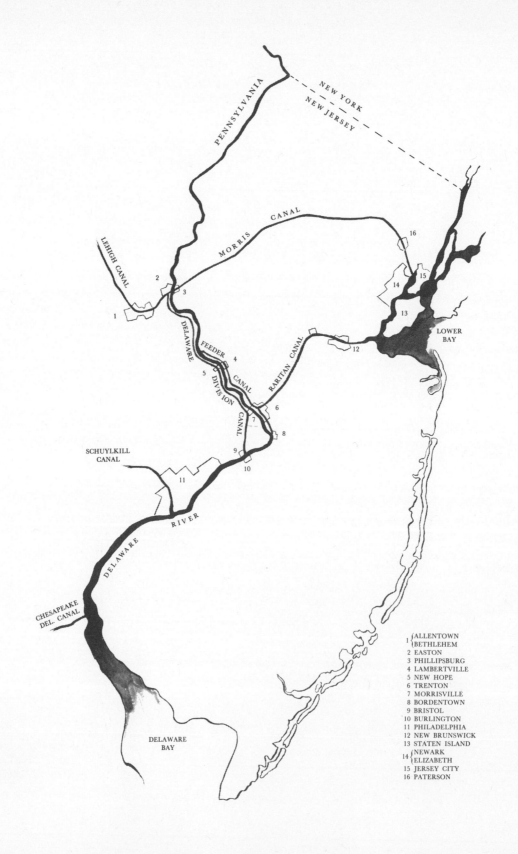

PENNSYLVANIA

NEW YORK

NEW JERSEY

LEHIGH CANAL

MORRIS   CANAL

16

15

14

13

LOWER
BAY

DELAWARE

FEEDER

DIVISION

CANAL

RARITAN CANAL

12

1

2

3

4

5

6

7

8

9

10

SCHUYLKILL
CANAL

11

RIVER

DELAWARE

CHESAPEAKE
DEL. CANAL

DELAWARE
BAY

1 { ALLENTOWN
  { BETHLEHEM
2 EASTON
3 PHILLIPSBURG
4 LAMBERTVILLE
5 NEW HOPE
6 TRENTON
7 MORRISVILLE
8 BORDENTOWN
9 BRISTOL
10 BURLINGTON
11 PHILADELPHIA
12 NEW BRUNSWICK
13 STATEN ISLAND
14 { NEWARK
   { ELIZABETH
15 JERSEY CITY
16 PATERSON

LEHIGH COAL & NAVIGATION Co.
CANAL DEPARTMENT.
LOCATION of LOCKS and TABLE of DISTANCES.

LOCK NUMBER		NEAREST STATION. on C.R.R. or N.J.	APPROXIMATE DISTANCE FROM MAUCH CHUNK		REMARKS. LEHIGH DIVISION
	COALPORT	MAUCH CHUNK		1.44 or 1½ Mile	COALPORT COAL POCKETS
1	U.S. 2	"	0.91 or 1 Mile		HEAD OF DAM Nº 1. U.S. "PACKER'S DAM."
2	U.S. 1	"	0.72 " ¾ "		FOOT OF DAM Nº 1. U.S. "PACKER'S DAM."
	MAUCH CHUNK			0.14 or ¼ Mile	
3	GUARD 1	"	0.00 " 0 "	0.00 0 "	FOOT OF DAM Nº1. " MAUCH CHUNK DAM "
4	WEIGH & 2	"	0.31 " ½ "		TWIN LOCKS
5	3	"	0.76 " ¾ "		L.V.R.R. BRIDGE CROSSES
6	4	"	1.18 " 1¼ "		FOOT OF "DEEP LEVEL"
7	5	"	1.60 " 1½ "		PACKERTON - OPPOSITE
8	6	"	1.81 " 1¾ "		
9	7	WEISSPORT	2.77 " 2¾ "		FOOT OF "LONG RUN LEVEL"
10	8	"	3.48 " 3½ "		BOAT YARD.
	WEISSPORT			3.70 or 3¾	
11	9	"	3.83 " 3¾ "		
12	10	"	4.27 " 4¼ "		
13	11	PARRYVILLE	4.83 " 4¾ "		½ MILE WEST OF FURNACE.
14	13	"	5.50 " 5½ "		HEAD OF PARRYVILLE DAM.
	PARRYVILLE			5.54 or 5½	
15	GUARD 2	BOWMANS	6.32 " 6¼ "		FOOT OF PARRYVILLE DAM.
	BOWMANS			6.84 or 6¾	
16	15	"	7.04 " 7 "		½ MILE EAST OF BOWMANS STAT.
17					

9.84
3.70
6.14

6 ¼

66	8	"	81.05 " 81 "		
	OUTLET	"		81.05 or 81	OUTLET TO DELAWARE RIVER.
67	PAPER MILL LOCK	"	81.25 " 81¼ "		
	WHEELS	"		81.29 or 81¼	POWER WHEELS. NEW HOPE.
	BROWNSBURG	MOORE		84.06 or 84	
	TAYLORSVILLE	WASHINGTON'S CROSSING		87.25 or 87¼	DELAWARE RIVER BRIDGE - TOLL
68	7	SCUDDER'S FALLS	89.66 " 89¾ "		
69	6		90.28 " 90¼ "		
	YARDLEY	WILBURTHA		91.18 or 91¼	DELAWARE RIVER BRIDGE - TOLL.
70	5	ASYLUM	91.82 " 91¾ "		
	MORRISVILLE	TRENTON		95.69 or 95¾	DELAWARE RIVER BRIDGE - TOLL.
	PENN VALLEY	PENN VALLEY		98.05 or 98	
	TULLYTOWN	TULLYTOWN		100.64 or 100¾	
71	4	"	102.53 " 102½ "		
72	3	BRISTOL	104.70 " 104¾ "		
73	2		104.80 " 104¾ "		
	BRISTOL			104.84 or 104¾	
74	1		104.96 " "		
75	TIDE LOCK	"	105.12 " 105 "		OUTLET TO DELAWARE RIVER.

NOTE: TOTAL DISTANCE COALPORT TO TIDE LOCK AT BRISTOL, 106.56 or 106½ MILES.
TOTAL NUMBER OF THROUGH LOCKS. 75
DISTANCES GIVEN ARE FROM GUARD LOCK Nº1, MAUCH CHUNK, PA.

CORRECT:- *Wm B. Spengler*   APPROVED:- *E.H. Shipman*
ASSIST. ENGR.   CANAL SUPERINTENDENT.

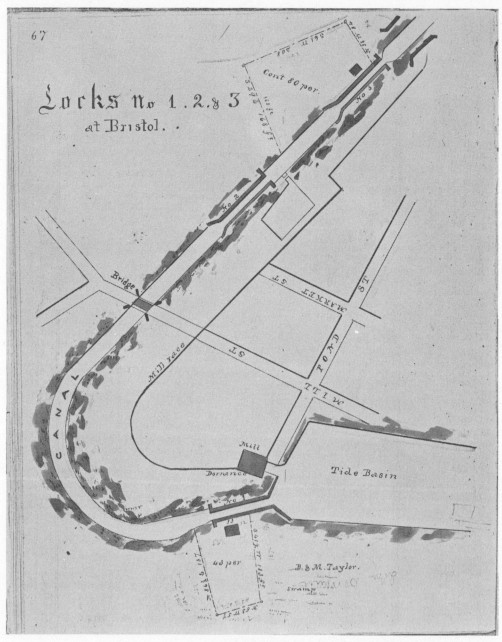

67

Locks № 1 . 2 .₃ 3
at Bristol . .

Three locks constituted the Bristol area. Here the Canal made a half circle, the purpose of which was to keep the flow of water slower and not let it empty out into the Tide Water Basin. The Basin would hold 100 boats at a time. All this has long since disappeared; as Bristol grew the canal became lost. Section after section was filled and industry covered what was once a boat basin and canal waterway. Records of Penna. Dept. of Forests & Waters, early engineer's drawing.

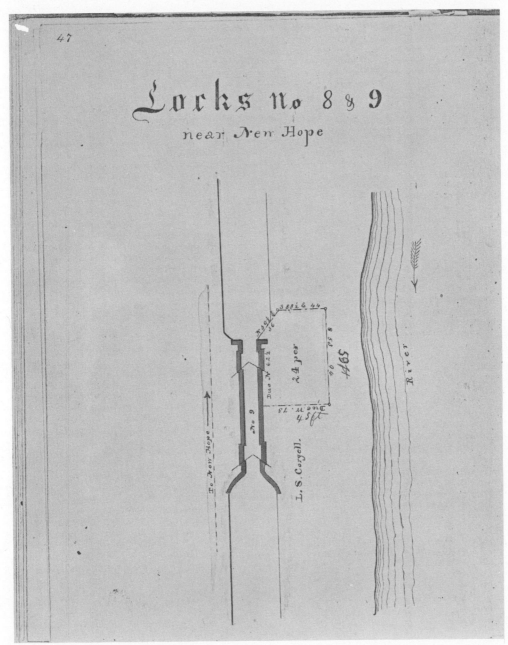

Lock No. 9 — At this point the collector's office and weighing of boats was performed, also between 9 and 10 the lumber yard where small boat repairs were made.

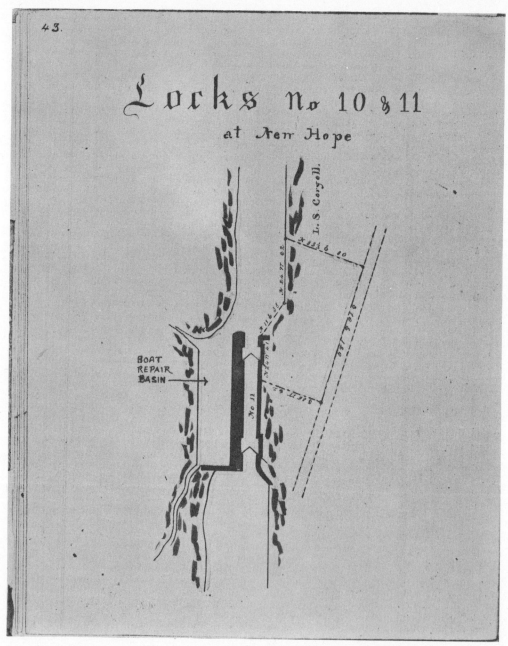

Locks no 10 & 11
at New Hope

Lock No. 11 is the first lock on entering New Hope southbound to Bristol. Barge parties now use this area for trips up and back in a barge. No. 10 is just below, also a double lock like No. 11. This lock was removed when road changes were made recently. Engineer's diagram only showed one lock when two close together were of same construction.

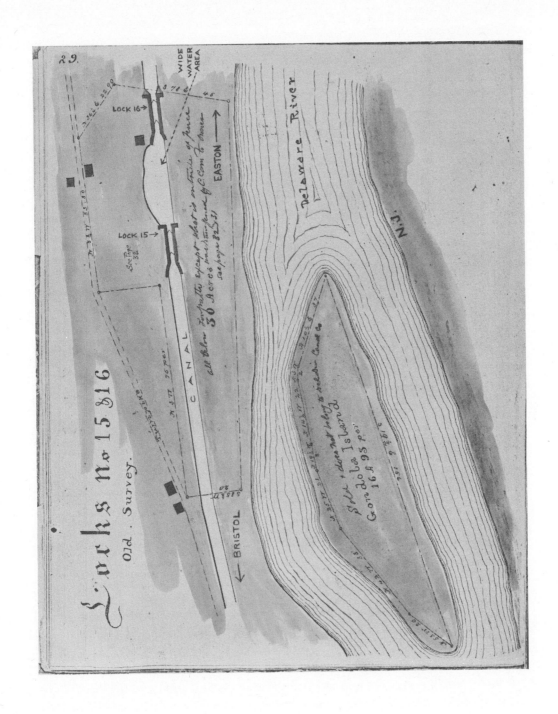

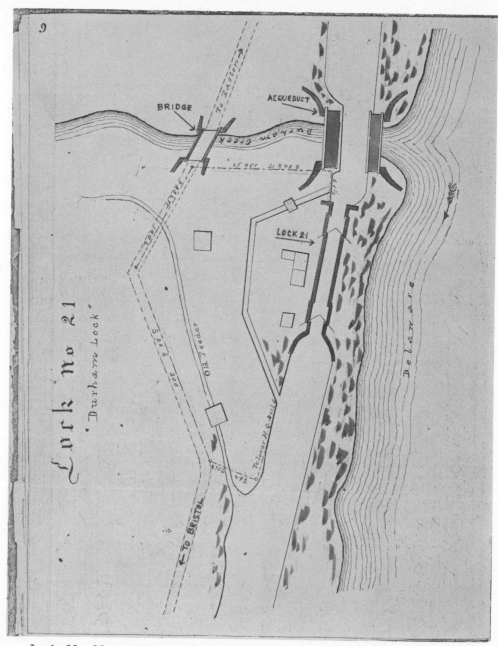

Locks No. 22 and 23 were between Easton and No. 21, where the Durham Creek crosses the Canal, an aqueduct takes the canal water above and over the Durham Creek. Just a short distance below the aqueduct is Lock No. 21 known as Durham Lock.

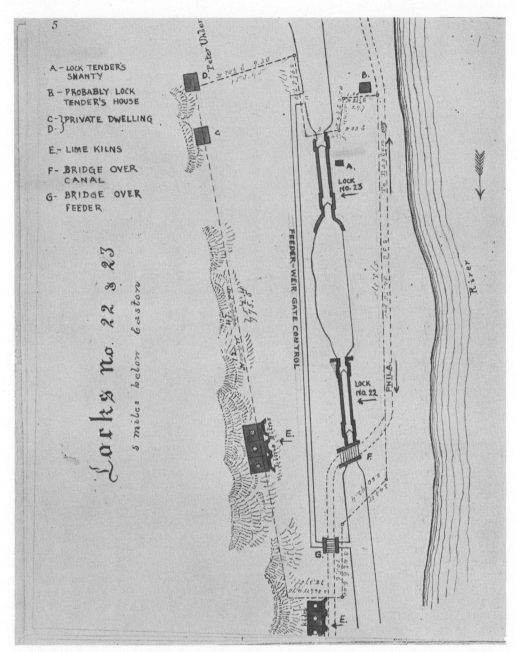

The old survey renderings, with number in corners, are the original ones made for the plan study of Delaware Division Canal construction. *Note:* the locks indicate wicket type gates at both ends. This was changed and a fall gate was used on the north end (upper end of lock). The wicket gate was placed at the lower end (south).

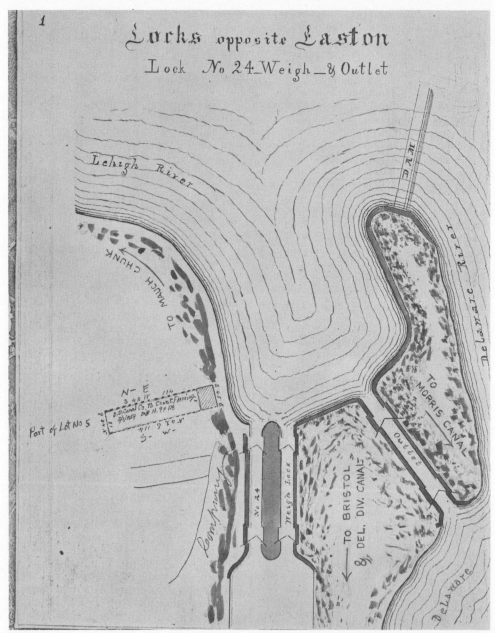

Locks opposite Easton
Lock No 24 _ Weigh _ & Outlet

The dam across the mouth of the Lehigh River helps hold back this great source of water supply, feeding it to the three sets of locks. The outlet lock allows boats to leave the Lehigh River and enter the Delaware River, where they cross to the Morris Canal. Lock No. 24 and Weigh Lock, transfer the boats into the Delaware Division Canal as they leave the Lehigh. Coming back into the Lehigh this operation would be the same except reverse direction.

PLEASURE BOAT (Other than Canoe or Row Boat) TOLLS.

Distance Limits. Miles.	Season Ticket.		Monthly Ticket.	
	Lockage not included.	Lockage included.	Lockage not included.	Lockage included.
1 to 11..........	$15.00	$ 25.00	$ 5.00	$ 8.00
12 to 25..........	....	30.00	....	10.00
26 to 40..........	....	40.00	....	12.00
41 to 55..........	....	50.00	....	14.00
56 to 70..........	....	65.00	....	17.00
71 to 85..........	....	80.00	....	20.00
86 to 106..........	....	100.00	....	25.00

Where a SEASON or MONTHLY ticket indicates on its face (in red) that lockage is not included, and the boat indicated thereon passes through a lock, a charge of twenty-five (25) cents additional shall be made by the lock-tender in charge, for each such lockage.

The above named rates will include the LAUNCH TENDER OR TRAILER, in tow of the launch or when carried on deck.

ONE WAY AND ROUND TRIP TOLLS FOR PLEASURE BOATS.
OTHER THAN CANOES OR ROW BOATS.

CHARGE.

1. BOAT TOLL, three (3) cents per mile for distance the permit is issued.

2. PASSENGER TOLL, ¼c per mile per passenger for distance the permit is issued.

   NOTE.—Two (2) persons are allowed free toll, being considered boat crew, all others are to be considered passengers.

3. LOCKAGE CHARGE. The following additional charges are to be made for lockage when the boat in its journey requires,

   1 to 5 lockages, charge—25 cents per lockage.

   6 to 10 lockages, charge—20 cents per lockage.

   11 to 20 lockages, charge—15 cents per lockage.

   21 to 30 lockages, charge—10 cents per lockage.

   31 and over,   charge— 5 cents per lockage.

PERMITS.

Total of above items 1, 2 and 3 will, therefore, constitute the full charge to be collected for a single, or one-way-trip, for which the permit is issued.

A round trip permit is issued at double the one-way charge (items 1 and 2), plus the charge for lockage (as per item 3) at the rate noted for the total number of lockages made in said round trip.

CANOE AND ROW BOAT TOLLS.

Distance Limits. Miles.	Season Ticket. Lockage not included.	Monthly Ticket. Lockage not included.
1 to 11..........	$ 2.00	$ 1.00
12 to 25..........	3.00	1.50
26 to 40..........	4.00	2.00
41 to 55..........	5.00	2.50
56 to 70..........	6.00	3.00
71 to 85..........	7.00	3.50
86 to 106..........	8.00	4.00

ONE-WAY and ROUND TRIP TOLL for Canoes or Row Boats. Charge, one (1) cent per mile for the distance the permit is issued. (A round trip toll constitutes double the one-way charge.)
CANOES CANNOT BE PASSED THROUGH ANY LOCK, EITHER SINGLY OR WITH OTHER CRAFT, BUT MUST BE CARRIED AROUND LOCKS.
NOTE.—Row Boats, too heavy to be carried around locks, may be locked through at the same rate for lockage as is provided in this tariff applying to launches.
All single or round trip permits must be surrendered to Collector or Locktender at the end of journey.
Permits can be obtained at the offices of Collectors at Bristol, New Hope, Mauch Chunk; at the Superintendent's Office, South Bethlehem, Pa., and at the Canal Traffic Manager's Office, Philadelphia, Pa.

The Lehigh Coal and Navigation Company rate schedule, 1914.

ROBERT J. McCLELLAN was born in Hopewell, New Jersey, in 1906. Leaving high school in his sophomore year, he began the self-education that has included such activities as railroad section hand, plumber's helper, paperhanger, textile weaver, boxing instructor, and sporting goods salesman. He found his vocation when the Curtis Publishing Company employed him as a special apprentice in their experimental gravure plant and trained him as a four-color retouch artist. This experience was the turning point in his life, starting both his career in the printing industry and his avocation of painter.

In his forty years as a gravure artist, Mr. McClellan has made more than one thousand four-color separations. Meanwhile, he has continued studying, practicing, and teaching in the fine arts. His work has received numerous awards and about four hundred of his paintings are hung in galleries or private collections.

Mr. McClellan's home and studio are on the Delaware Canal at New Hope.

Princeton Public Library
Princeton, New Jersey
www.princetonlibrary.org
609.924.9529

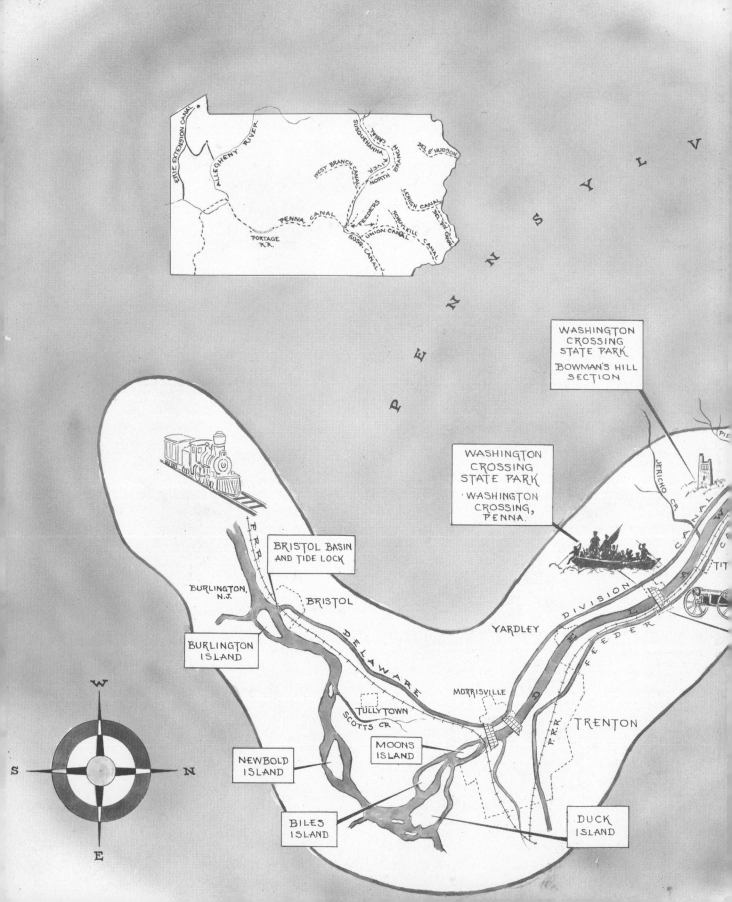